Tasting Wisdom

Tasting Wisdom

A Daily Companion for Meditation

Laurence Freeman

CANTERBURY
PRESS

© Laurence Freeman 2025

Published in 2025 by Canterbury Press
Editorial office
3rd Floor, Invicta House,
110 Golden Lane,
London EC1Y 0TG, UK
www.canterburypress.co.uk

Canterbury Press is an imprint of Hymns Ancient & Modern Ltd
(a registered charity)

Hymns Ancient & Modern® is a registered trademark of
Hymns Ancient & Modern Ltd
13A Hellesdon Park Road, Norwich,
Norfolk NR6 5DR, UK

Scripture quotations taken from the New English Bible, copyright © Cambridge
University Press and Oxford University Press 1961, 1970. All rights reserved.

British Library Cataloguing in Publication data

A catalogue record for this book is available
from the British Library

ISBN: 978-1-78622-653-2

EU GPSR Authorised Representative
LOGOS EUROPE, 9 rue Nicolas Poussin, 17000, LA ROCHELLE, France
E-mail: Contact@logoseurope.eu

Typeset by Regent Typesetting
Printed and bound by
CPI Group (UK) Ltd

Contents

For Barry White in gratitude

Acknowledgements

Selecting and compiling these 366 entries was made a much lighter task thanks to the response of a multitude of those who receive my Daily Wisdom photo and email online.

When we asked for their favourite Daily Wisdoms, we were amazed by the response from so many and so quickly. These had to be edited as most were from transcripts of my talks but it was a great help to get started. Thank you, daily wisdomites, and Kevin Wittoeck for coordinating the process.

To sign up for the Daily Wisdom to your email, to WCCM updates and other communications go to:

wccm.org/mailings/

Preface

Reading a menu is informative, and a good one will stimulate desire and expectation. But it is still not eating and tasting the food. So, too, thinking of ideas in the spiritual domain may prepare us for the experience but are by no means the experience itself. If organised religion today has lost so much credibility and authority it may be because the whole dimension of religious or spiritual experience has fallen to such a low level, especially at a time when people are so hungry for the experience. The low priority given by churches, seminaries and religious teaching generally to contemplative experience has resulted in an exodus into the wilderness for many. It recalls the warning of Jesus: 'You are the salt to the world. If salt becomes tasteless, how is its saltiness to be restored?' (Matt. 5.13).

That is an urgent question today. It affects most of the psychological and social aspects of the painful multiple crises we are passing through. Is it a downward spiral ending in self-destruction on a grand scale? Or can we see it (and so make it) to be a dark evolutionary night of the human soul out of the tunnel of which we will emerge? Hopefully what awaits will justify Shakespeare's optimism: 'What a piece of work is a man! How Noble in reason! How infinite in faculty! In form and moving how express and admirable! In Action, how like an Angel in apprehension, how like a God!' (*Hamlet* II:2)

Who knows? Life is uncertain. But in times like ours we become acutely aware of what this means. Then we easily lose peace and reason by endlessly over-speculating about what might happen next. The solution, I think, is to focus on the next thing we should do and do it. Of course, there are many things we should do next in the right order but even getting these in perspective is difficult if we are sinking into chronic anxiety and fear.

In these daily readings I am focusing on one thing. That does not mean it is the only thing but it makes a big difference. That is our next meditation period as the next thing to do. Daily meditation, ideally twice a day, morning and evening. This is challenging because it sometimes seems as if nothing happens in the meditation. Silence, stillness, simplicity are happening. But if you feel discouraged you may read one of these daily entries and perhaps perceive your experience differently. Or recall Beckett's hopeful pessimism: 'Try again. Fail again. Fail better.' This could also be seen as the wisdom of humility.

Wisdom is the salt of living. With the loss of wisdom, life seems tasteless, meaningless. Tasting wisdom restores zest for life. The Latin word for wisdom is *sapientia,* from an ancient root meaning to taste or perceive. Meditation is a universal practice capable of healing the wounds of polarisation and conflict with the salt of wisdom. Meditating daily is tasting wisdom every day. If this book can help get you started or restarted when you stop on this path, I will think it has been well worthwhile putting together for you.

Laurence Freeman
Bonnevaux
October 2024

January

1 January

THERE IS A difference between seeing and looking at. In meditation we are not looking at God because God is never an object. Nor are we looking at ourselves – as we usually do. It is something excitingly, strangely different: pure vision, seeing itself.

2 January

WE ARE ENTERING what early Christian teachers called 'pure prayer'. Pure because it is simple and uncorrupted. It filters the heart of images, desires, fears – and all complexity. The true test of purity is simplicity.

3 January

USUALLY, WE DON'T like people to see how odd we are; but that very oddness is the opening into our true value.

4 January

SOMEWHERE WE EACH fit into the great jigsaw puzzle. Without our fitting in, the universe itself is not complete.

HIS CONTINUOUS PRESENCE, within the absence created by his death, is the essential message of the gospel.

THE GOAL OF life – whether it is called heaven, nirvana, moksha, salvation or enlightenment – is not separate from knowing fully who we are.

SELF-TRANSCENDENCE IS the way to self-knowledge just as death leads into fuller life.

OUR JOURNEY TO self-knowledge is unique but is made within the mundane tasks and responsibilities of life. The ground we walk on each day is holy ground.

9 January

SELF-KNOWLEDGE IS A transformative knowing, moving us rapidly along the full spectrum of human growth. It changes all the worlds we inhabit or visit along the way.

10 January

MEDITATION AND FRIENDSHIP have this in common: each leads us directly to know who we are. They bring us to self-knowledge, which is always a mystery. 'Who am I?' is a lifelong question. And because it is such a serious question, we must approach it with a good degree of humour.

11 January

JOY AND SUFFERING are twin experiences of life when it is lived as a spiritual journey. Suffering comes in facing and overcoming our inner demons. Each of us has at least one major demon to confront. If we embrace the transcendent conditions of the inner place of prayer, not evading what we are there to do, then the journey acquires value and meaning. Even in suffering, joy happens when we forget ourselves.

12 January

IN THE DEATH of the teacher, a disciple meets fully, in absence and silence, the teaching he had previously heard mainly in the mind.

ACCEPT OURSELVES AS we are, with our faults, weaknesses and odd tendencies and then we also *know* ourselves by understanding what it is we are accepting. It is not enough just to accept ourselves. To accept ourselves unconditionally means to know ourselves. Then, as we know ourselves, we see beyond ourselves. We see how we are not limited to this particular egocentric persona that we identify with. We are greater and humbler than that because our true centre is not in ourselves but in God.

HOW DO WE love ourselves? We love ourselves by becoming still. Stillness is a great discipline; it is the great discovery of meditation. Stillness becomes the dynamic of transcendence. The more still we are, the more we transcend our limitations. Now, stillness does not mean stopping. It is not static. We fully experience stillness when we feel how it is part of the whole process of growth in nature. There is a wondrous relationship between stillness and growth.

15 January

THE EGO IS dissolved only by love, by opening itself to what lies beyond it, to that true light of which the ego is only a blurred reflection. We cannot love without poverty, which means letting go. We cannot love ourselves without entering into poverty of spirit. This is the first step: giving up, renouncing the patterns of control and ego-effort, in which we have become addictively, unconsciously enmeshed.

16 January

IN THE MUNDANE things of daily life, we come to find that the background radiation of love, the all-present power of God, is constant and everywhere.

17 January

EXPERIENCING RELATIONSHIP AT the level of our true self involves moving beyond any vestige of duality or separateness. If I meet *you* in this kingdom of the true self, then we are not conscious of separation; we are conscious in union, in love. This is how every follower of Jesus tastes the fruit of meditation practised in faith. Pure prayer deepens our knowledge and our love of Christ.

18 January

YOU MIGHT BE completely unaware of what's going on around you, totally blind to people's needs. Or you might observe those needs but fail to give them your attention. When awareness develops into attention, and attention is always personal, then you move from a kind of basic animal aware-ness into human attention in which we experience compassion and so know the source of compassion.

COMPASSION ARISES FIRST out of awareness. It is natural; you don't need to be a saint to feel it for somebody
suffering. But it is attention, personal attention, which trans-
lates awareness into attention and spontaneous action and,
therefore, into real relationship.

WHEN WE MEDITATE, we are entering the quality of
prayer that early Christians called *pure prayer*. It purifies
the heart of all images, desires and fears. It unties the complexity associated with those things. What is pure is simple. We
often say something is 'pure and simple'. So, when we meditate,
we are not speaking to God; we are not thinking about God
in a complex way; we are not bringing our problems to God's
door and pinning them up on his noticeboard. Being simple
means that we are not dramatising our relationship with God
by asking for problems to be solved or desires fulfilled. The
purity and simplicity of meditation is contemplation which
resolves problems by giving us a new understanding of them.

IN THE PRACTICE of meditation we do not allow our
petitions or intentions to enter into the pure prayer. 'God
knows our needs even before we ask.' But we *are* paying
attention. Not making intentions but giving attention. This is
the pure seeing of meditation, of the contemplative state. It is
the vision of God, the *seeing* of God. So, we do not entertain
particular ideas, images or theories of God in our mind. We
are not *speaking to God*, we are not thinking about our problems. We are doing something greater: we are *being in and
with* God.

22 January

TO MEDITATE, YOU have to practise attention, which is
why many people give it up too soon: paying attention can
be hard work. As you read this now, you may also be thinking of dinner with friends or a problem at work. You may be
also saying, 'Oh, I shouldn't be thinking of that now; I should
be thinking of these great thoughts that old Whatshisname
is sharing.' But when we do pay attention to what someone,
anyone, is saying – or listen to the mantra – we quickly discover that attention is good work. It brings out the best in
us and it produces benefits for others. Any kind of attention
involves leaving self behind, because in giving your attention
you are *giving* yourself.

T HE BASIC THEOLOGY of all Christian prayer is that the journey of prayer is beyond our own prayer, beyond 'my' egocentric prayer, and leads into the prayer of Christ himself: 'I live no longer but Christ lives in me ... We do not know how to pray but the Spirit prays within us.' Meditation puts that to the proof.

M EDITATION, OR 'PURE prayer' as the Desert Teachers called it, takes us beyond thought and so ultimately beyond the ego. It prepares us for the next step, which is the result of grace, not just our effort: the final step from ourselves into the Mind of Christ which plunges us into God. John Cassian, a Desert Father and teacher of this prayer, shows how it is interrelated to all the other kinds of prayer. You do not have to give up any other useful spiritual practice when you make meditation an integral part of your life. But be prepared for change anywhere when the time comes.

J OHN MAIN SPEAKS of meditation as a way of faith. He sees it as a leap of faith that we make towards the Other, towards God, 'before the other appears and with no pre-packaged guarantee that the other will appear'. He explains this as 'the risk involved in all loving'. Faith is inextricably connected to loving. Meditation will show you what faith means. In the Christian tradition it is also understood as a way of love with the outcome of becoming more and more loving.

THE TEST THAT our meditation is getting us somewhere is not how high we levitate, psychic gifts we develop or experiences we may have in the meditation period. The real test of meditation is how we answer: 'Are we becoming a more loving person?' As with any repeated act of faith, meditation deepens our capacity for faith and becomes a way of life. Humanity expands by becoming more faithful. Modern culture speaks much about human growth but often misses that faith (not belief) is at the heart of being human. We can look at our experiences and wonder: 'Is this going to be a growth experience? What am I going to learn through this?' We might better ask: will this make me more faithful?

GROWTH IS INDEED a test of authenticity. Life always has some meaning. Even in painful loss or other suffering we are growing in faith, growing into love. Without our sensing the meaning of experience, we can miss the opportunity for faith, becoming just a flash in the dark, a fleeting glimpse of the mystery. But when experience is embedded in faith, in love, in communion and supported in a living tradition, it becomes transparent, diaphanous vision. Not just a blinking glimpse but seeing.

JOHN MAIN SAID that every time we sit to meditate, we are entering a tradition. Faith is experience of tradition as living transmission. Tradition doesn't mean a freezer-fresh set of beliefs, structures or rituals. It is not something frozen in time. Tradition: the word literally means a 'passing or handing on', as in a relay race. Done well it is passing on, without dropping the baton of wisdom, sure knowledge and greater capacity for faith.

29 January

ONE OF THE typical phrases of the Desert Monastics is heard when a younger monk approaches an elder, a spiritual mother or father, and says: 'Give me a word by which I may live.' We find this often in the 'Conferences of the Fathers' that John Cassian wrote in the early fifth century after leaving Egypt to bring the wisdom of the desert, including meditation, to the West. He came to Marseilles, not so far from Bonnevaux, and founded a double monastery of men and women. His work offered the order of wisdom to a wild, anarchic time of social breakdown, not so different from ours. We too need to be seeking words of wisdom.

30 January

FOR THE CONTEMPLATIVE, Christian prayer is not, essentially, speaking to God, or thinking about God. It is about entering a unique, wordless, thought-free, silent 'conversation' with God enabled for us in the Mind of Christ. It is not about negotiating between our will and God's, or flattering him to get what we want, or asking him to change his mind. Does God change his mind? Prayer is pure action, a wholehearted surrender to the love of God who already knows our needs with a uniquely intimate love because he participates directly in our humanity, sharing in all our woundedness, doubt and complexity. Surrender? Kind of, but a triumphant surrender, not a defeat.

31 January

OF COURSE, LIFE is stressful. Life changes daily but has an expiry date. Anything as unpredictable as human existence has to be seen in terms of probabilities. Life's uncertain nature is never easy to accept until we have fully accepted the nature of uncertainty. The real problem, then, is not stress but whether we can handle the stress points of life with the peace that comes from total acceptance of things as they are. If we suffer stress without this deep alignment with reality, stress will feed off itself and grow out of control. Then the main false god Mammon tries to deceive us into thinking that the greater the stress, the more we are subjected to those other false gods called Success and Failure.

February

THE DYING EXPERIENCE that meditation leads us into, like every taste of death, involves separation. This separation is a component of all the many kinds of death experience. It is also an essential part of our coming to wholeness. We begin to learn the art of dying as we separate from the womb, from the breast, as we emotionally detach from parents, family and protective childhood institutions and especially when our hearts are broken. Each of these is a death experience involving both suffering and, eventually, expansion into new life.

FROM THE SPIRITUAL and especially from the Christian perspective, death is separation rather than extinction. Faith knows there is life after death. 'Keep death always before your eyes,' St Benedict advises. He means keep this essential process of life in the foreground, be conscious of it. Don't forget you are here to die and rise again. Never forget this is constantly happening. Prayer helps to keep this conscious and focuses all you are in it. There can be no meaning in life without death. To be conscious of the dying process, to 'keep it always before your eyes', will vitalise you and keep you resilient and awake.

EMBRACING DEATH, THE dying process of each day happens in pure prayer. It also prepares us for our last death, to meet death fearlessly as we breathe our last. It does this by revealing to us our true self, who we truly are. And there is no separation from the true self. In this core identity of our true self, we are eternally who we are: the unique, loved creation, emission, manifestation of God. In the true self there is no death. It is the meaning of Jesus who breathed his last, having learned how to die. And it is the meaning of Christ who cannot die again. He passed through the great separation from the ego which is the daily work of meditation. Like a rocket launching, some parts have to fall away to complete the launch. As we die, he is with us as we go through this same separation process.

TO REALLY BEGIN to meditate introduces us to reality in ways that are both challenging and wonderfully refreshing. It is great to discover that, at least in some moments of the day, you can be completely truthful, transparently honest. This requires giving up the illusion of perfectionism. You really begin when you recognise and accept that you do not need even to try to be a perfect meditator.

THE FIRST THING to be shed in the launch is the virus of perfectionism. If we don't detach we cannot rise. Perfectionism is an inherently judgemental state that generates the guilty feeling that we should aspire to be perfect: successful and perfect like gold-medal athletes, or holy like the saints we admire. This virus of perfectionism can be eradicated as was the smallpox virus. Daily meditation is like your antibiotic against the disease that has infected every ego. We may not even be aware we have it but the need to 'look good' affects us lifelong. The obsession with success is the first obstacle we confront because it is the most primitive opponent to our journey to wholeness. We need to confront it right at the beginning.

6 February

MEDITATION AND MEDICINE. The words are related through the prefix *med-* which connotes 'care' and 'attention'. Today this connection between the art of prayer and the art of healing illuminates the integration of spirituality with mental healthcare. It offers a major resource for restoring and sustaining mental health in a society as psychologically damaged and spiritually undernourished as ours. It teaches us how to transform the scourge of self-destructive loneliness into the wisdom of solitude. All this is part of realising the discovery, recognition and finally the acceptance of our uniqueness and our human destiny to be one with God.

7 February

DESPITE THE SOMEWHAT improved media image of the church under Pope Francis, it still faces the blank look of incomprehension when it uses its standard language in communicating with most secular people and especially with the young. First, it should connect with their often-unconscious hunger for meaning, showing they are understood. And second, it should introduce them to silence. Identify the real questions before giving the answers. This throws a bridge over the gulf of miscommunication. It is just the kind of bridge that the light-footed Holy Spirit can dance across.

8 February

FOR THE CONTEMPLATIVE Christian, prayer becomes an active, wholehearted surrender in faith to the incomprehensible love of God who knows our needs better than we do, because God is closer to us than we are to ourselves. For any serious meditator who doesn't have God in their vocabulary, the experience is the same. Who knows how or when they will interpret it?

9 February

THE EXPERIENCE OF God is more widespread than religious people usually imagine. The early Christians had enough sense of mystery to understand this. They said that, 'Whoever loves knows God; and whoever does not love cannot know God.' Love is the fruit of faith, not belief. This simple, revolutionary truth became buried in an intellectual competition to prove the existence of God and impose one kind of belief over others. My God is superior to yours. Kierkegaard, a very modern teacher of faith, said that the more we refine our proofs for God the less convincing they are.

10 February

TO THE MIND addicted to noise and novelty, silence seems like a negative emptiness. In reality, it *is* empty but also filled with an infinite degree of potential matching the level of silence attained. Ultimately, we fall over the edge, beyond boundaries, into an 'order without order', into the explosive freedom of the life of Spirit: the silence that *is* God. Meister Eckhart describes this in the mystical language of paradox when he said: 'In contemplation we become pregnant with nothing and in the nothing God is born. God begets His Son in our soul. God begets me as His Son.'

11 February

SELF-KNOWLEDGE IS NOT stuff we learn about ourselves through magazine questionnaires. It is what we lose – and re-find in a different way – in solitude. This kind of self-knowledge cannot be reduced to algorithms or frozen into concepts. We see it in its effects, all the changes self-knowledge makes in life. As we become still and loosen the grip of the ego, things change. Not under our control but as they are meant to change. A kind of knowledge we have not known before gently rises in us. It can cause turbulence, as all change does, but in itself it is gentle. As in the story of Elijah's encounter with God on the holy mountain, it comes with a power of gentle quietness and modesty that is stronger than an earthquake or a hurricane.

12 February

THE SENSE THAT we have been chosen unsettles us. I don't mean like winning *X-Factor* or joining a cult. Sensing a destiny that we are free to accept or reject still threatens the ego and may force us into hostility towards whoever it is doing the choosing. But learning a contemplative wisdom (how else except through discipline?) helps us to handle change and to see that to be authentically chosen and to consent is the greatest liberation.

13 February

THE KINGDOM IS not a place we are going to nor a reward for being good. The Kingdom is the real, not imagined, presence of God. Where is it? Jesus says: 'You cannot observe when the Kingdom of God will come. You cannot say, "Look, here it is or there it is", because in fact the Kingdom of Heaven is within you.' The word translated as 'within' means 'among' or 'in your midst'. So, the Kingdom transcends all opposites by revealing their point of union. It is unlimited by space or time. One more thing it reveals is that real presence is reciprocal.

14 February

AS I SEE with the eye of the heart what is in me – 'Christ in you' – I no less experience it in others, in everyone I meet. I venture to say that faith in Jesus means being able to recognise him in each other, in his mysterious form that discloses the Kingdom. When we are truly open to another in any human relationship, this is what we see in the other person. It then intensifies who and what we see in ourselves.

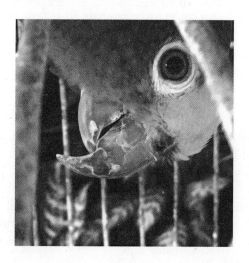

15 February

THE CONNECTION BETWEEN the historical Jesus and the Inner Christ is the most fascinating, mysterious, exciting and continuous process in my life. To feel I'm connected to it intensifies my sense of connection to everything in this world. Through that connection, I can sense and love the truth in every religious tradition and in the individuals who manifest the heart of that tradition. I have come to believe that to be a Christian is a constantly unfolding process, not at all a fixed identity. It is an evolution, what Gregory of Nyssa called endless growth. It means there is no competition and no rejection. Jesus did not compete with other spiritual leaders, so why should his followers compete or claim to be 'saved' while others are condemned? It is hardly Christlike to do that.

16 February

WE CAN NEVER know God by thought alone. As unknowing leads us into the heart and fuller silence, the 'question that has no answer' resolves into pure prayer. Unknowing is faith and faith becomes love. We only know God by love. The intelligence of the heart is love. So, God is no longer a problem. The problem becomes an encounter with unsuspected levels of reality, released not in gnostic realms but into all the events and encounters of our lives. We find the answer there – as John Main says – 'in our own experience'. Prayer illuminates the meaning in our experience.

17 February

WE KNOW GOD in our self-knowledge because it transcends everything we think we know of ourselves. As Sufi mystics and those who recognise the Risen Christ understand, God disguises himself as ourselves. Or, as Simone Weil who knew Christ said, 'He comes to us hidden and salvation consists in our recognising him.'

MEDITATION PREPARES US to receive the gift. John Main said it is the way we 'accept the gift of our being' and all it is made of. It can be discouraging to see what slow learners we are. But only failure teaches us this, so we should never undervalue the gift that is failure. We may respond to the gift and see the fruits growing. Yet so easily, like a rubber band frightened of breaking, we snap back, into the default system of egocentricity. The deep breathing of other-centredness is interrupted again. We may risk sharing ourselves with another person. When it fails to evoke the response we want, we pull back, ending unconditionality and starting to harden our hearts against further rejection or disappointment. Accepting failure helps us to find hope again.

19 February

HOW CAN WE reflect on the birth of Jesus without linking it to the Resurrection? Understanding is not transformed just by reflection but by a flash of recognition. Not just by trying to re-enter the past but by knowing the present. Gradual or sudden, the recognition of the Risen Christ is the transformation of the self.

20 February

HOW DO WE know our mind is calming? Simply because, even in situations of stress, confusion or fear, we are conscious of peace, joy and clarity, confirming to us that truth is within us. Although we can forget or reject it, it never abandons us. Come back to meditation after an extended time of dropping the practice or being unfaithful to anything where love resides. You will see that, once your initial self-doubting impulses of guilt and the fear of rejection are done with, a heart-breaking, wholehearted homecoming dawns and a celebratory feast of love awaits us. Read the parable of the Prodigal Son.

21 February

GRADUALLY THE LIFE of continuous prayer rises and permeates all our thought and action. Like St Patrick we find Christ as we walk, sleep, rise and work. Even in the midst of urban stress, waiting for trains, sitting in traffic jams, dealing with bureaucracy, hanging on the line and maddeningly being thanked for our exhausted patience, the deep calm mind is aware of the rising agitation and begins to defuse it. This is the wonderful understanding of prayer in Christian wisdom: 'I am with you always till the end of time.' It is also a practical necessity for human survival in the world of division and agitation that we have created for ourselves.

22 February

THE MANTRA FOCUSES the timeless mystery lived in daily life. Saying it is an act of unity, an expression of love that originates with a new kind of love for one's self. It seems like tough love at first but it expands into the Trinitarian experience itself – love of God, love of others, love of self. It leads to a divine harmony in oneself, healing the divided and conflicted dualities of the agitated mind: 'Do I want this or that or both? That person is my enemy. I desire this pleasure at any cost.' As all this dividedness is repaired in the mind we merge into the Trinitarian heart through a secret, intimate oneness with the humanity of Christ.

23 February

THE IDEA OF being rewarded appears often in the para-bles. But it is there as short-hand, not to be taken literally. Crucifixion shows what reward and punishment mean in God's eyes. To stand at the foot of the Cross – to be present to human suffering we cannot help – frees us from the false conclusions of the ego by exposing its fake colours. Reading between the lines of the teaching using the reward–punishment model frees us from fake news and from the identical twins of desire and fear. Being rewarded or being punished are metaphors for the natural law of karma. God transcends it because he neither rewards nor punishes. We do. Life does. But 'the Father shines on good and bad alike' and is kind to the ungrateful and the wicked. Stick with this teaching because the ego and the left brain do not like it one little bit.

24 February

IF WE AVOID looking for reward and give up trying to win approval, we stand a good chance of getting onto the wavelength of the spirit. Like super phone networks, this wave-length operates globally, connecting our spirit to the spirit of Christ and his to the spirit of God. Eventually we find a stable connection. In the joy of being universally interconnected, we see what ethical behaviour and divine love mean. 'In this breakthrough,' says Meister Eckhart, 'I discover that God and I are one.'

25 February

THE AMERICAN DECLARATION of Independence is more focused on independence than interdependence. It proclaims that every individual possesses 'inalienable' rights. It doesn't say how they transform the individual to participate responsibly in the whole. I have the right to bear arms, the right to life, liberty and the pursuit of happiness. But if I defend these rights universally the sharing goes beyond individualism to inter-being. We see with the tragic regularity of American mass killings in schools and malls how an individual's right to carry weapons can be misinterpreted and abused. What if we started by saying I have no rights that do not include the duty to defend the rights of others? What could bring about a mass metanoia to prevent the mass killings?

26 February

DAILY MEDITATION INTRODUCES us to the spirit of discipline, self-control, altruism, fidelity, mindfulness and fearlessness. These are relational and touch all relationships. We master a technique. But we love a discipline. At first, we may want to master something just to earn a reward. As we come to love the discipline of the art, the reward is to become a disciple. In the person of Jesus in the Gospels we see a spiritual master turned humbly towards his source, his Father. At the heart of every teacher there is a disciple.

27 February

MY FRIEND SR Eileen O'Hea had a memorable phrase I am always moved by: 'Relationships are the sacred ground of our humanity.' She had a deep and gentle insight into all the aspects of relationship. Existentially speaking, how can we realistically see ourselves *not* embedded in relationship wherever we look or feel: historically, socially, emotionally, ecologically and cosmically? We only exist in an infinitely interrelated network of being. Spiritually, we are related to everything in this all-inclusive dimension – in the one who is one with the one and where all things recognise their unity.

28 February

ALL OF THE things we desire and seek to acquire and then protect give us a temporary sense of security and belonging: things like pleasure, acceptance by others, good health, fulfilment and recognition in life and work. Yet they all eventually fail to convince us that they equate with our true self. They are not who we *are*, only what we *have*. So, we live with the constant need for 'something else'. We are tempted to seek it where we looked and failed before. As soon as we see this and wonder what our next step should be, we should reduce our possessions and simplify our life.

29 February (leap year)

IN MANY TRADITIONS, 30 minutes is the recommended median length for a period of meditation in an active lifestyle. When you have a very active or agitated lifestyle, it may take about that amount of time just to get beyond the emotional turbulence and mental distraction. We may find ourselves in a truly peaceful state of attention for a few seconds of that half hour. That taste of the contemplative state can be of immense benefit and regular practice will intensify and extend it. It is highly beneficial and we return to activity in a fresher state of mind. That's just the way our minds are. If we want permanent, deeper peace and purer clarity of mind we will need to sit down with a friend or mentor and decide how to manage our time differently.

March

1 March

TRANSCENDING THE INSTINCTIVE impulse to take flight when things get difficult is part of our human development and spiritual growing up. It shapes character, strengthens resilience and integrates our personality. We can even see the value of such challenges because they mature us in empathy to be of greater service to others. By accepting our own fear or suffering we find the way into self-transcendence. From that comes a different kind of love, a more free and purer love, a new experience of what love is, more than we could reach without having grown in faith.

2 March

JUST AS WE cannot know God as an object, so we cannot know ourselves merely as an object of our self-perception. So, knowing ourselves begins with de-objectifying ourselves. How do we de-objectify ourselves? Simply by taking the attention off ourselves and stop thinking about ourselves. This is the work we do in meditation as we cease from solving problems and fantasising about alternatives to reality. Meditation is so simple, so radical because of this. The moment we sit down to meditate we have restarted the pilgrimage of self-knowledge. We are continuing to make the work of self-discovery the work of self-realisation. Soon, as we feel what we are doing, it becomes a source of true value in our life.

3 March

RAMANA MAHARSHI SAID: 'The ego is really a ghost with no form of its own, but feeding on any form it holds.' Ponder that. Your ego is a ghost that feeds on whatever situation it sees itself in. It uses every situation to take control. Like a bad smell, it gets in everywhere. Into any plan, every relationship, any good work you are doing. The ego is a hungry ghost sucking life from everything it can. The ego, Ramana says, is a ghost with no form or substance of its own and 'when sought for, it takes flight'. So, take heart, when you track the ego down, it disappears.

4 March

MEDITATION IS A way of silence and communion with others, of self-discovery and self-transcendence, of relationship and solitude, a way to read without words, to know without thought. By this kind of self-knowledge, the meditator comes to the threshold of the knowledge of God as we grow, without observing it, in union of consciousness with Jesus. This union asks nothing of us except to use the capacity it gives us to make a total gift of self. Daily meditation, in a Christian understanding, is deepening union with the Mind of Christ. It is subtle. We encounter the Risen Christ even before we recognise or can name him.

5 March

STARTING TO MEDITATE inaugurates a new way of living. It is less about mastering a technique than following a discipline and seeing everything afresh. With a growing experience of communion, oneness with self and others, it surpasses the boundaries of all dualism: the split between you and me, us and them. Most of us are deeply concerned about our relationships, even seeing them as the sacred element of our lives, and so it is through our way of relating that we first see the new way of living and seeing. A contemplative practice develops this, showing us that relationships as we usually think of them are evolving into, let's call it, unified consciousness.

6 March

MEDITATION RADICALLY CHANGES the way we understand God. So radically, that God may at some moments seem to disappear. It makes an impact on our human relationships. It can also be felt in how we experience ourselves as part of the natural world. The humanity of Jesus and his relationship to the universe are also drawn into this change of perception. People often describe the effect of meditation as like 'coming home'. At the same time, it's like knowing home for the first time.

7 March

IN ALL MYTHS, the basic human quest is for our true self. Who am I? Where do I come from? The quest takes the hero through reduction, defeat and renunciation. Major new achievements always entail losses and letting go if they are to guide us to the joyful arrival of homecoming. At that moment there is a startling recognition of the obvious: we are who we are and nothing else and we are here and nowhere else. The miracle doesn't stop there. Recognising ourselves (less self-conscious, more attentive to others, capable of wonder), we awaken to harmony with all – in every human being, including our foes, in plants, fish, birds, spiders, moons and galaxies.

8 March

TO IMAGINE WE are the centre of everything is a common delusion of creatures: like the delusion of Lucifer who refused to serve because he wanted to be equal to God. But only God who has no boundaries can be the centre of everything. God's centre is everywhere and his circumference is nowhere. To imagine ourselves at the centre is pathological, a mental confusion. Taken to extremes, it might lead to a psychiatric ward or to mindless violence against others or even to a tyrannical head of state. We are called to join God at the centre. By stages. We need to accept boundaries in order to move into the boundless. The quest moves us from a worldview with us at the centre to the real world of God's boundlessness.

9 March

TO MEDITATE HELPS us to live better. It shows us that being human is a personal, intimate work that plunges us into the grounding relationship of all life: the entwined relationship between God and ourselves (and everything else). Aware of this, we find how the work of silence is part of all this as well as the cosmic web of relationships we belong in. Nothing is separate. Of course, there are times when we get discouraged or feel isolated. Hell exists in these spaces. But there are also times when we see the fruits of our labours and we know that Heaven lasts while Hell does not. Given this range of experience, it is clear why we need to be grounded in the deepest and most primal relationship of all.

10 March

I WAS JUST TALKING to somebody who has been meditating for some time but for whom the important penny has only just dropped: 'Oh, so I don't have to think about the meaning of the mantra as I say it.' I was surprised, and so were they, that it had taken them so long to really *get* what they must have *heard* many times: 'Meditation is not what you think.' Hearing it is not enough. It has to *happen* in us. What matters is the experience. It comes in its own time. At a certain degree of silence, experience and teaching become one.

11 March

AS WE LET go of words and thoughts, we are pilgrims from mind to heart. We come to places where only the Spirit teaches and leads into silence. It is a vitalising, awakening silence, not reverie or passive or negative. It is the light-filled silence of a communion of love. It is awakened whenever we experience that we are in God as the ground of being and with each other in love. The journey from mind to heart is filled and guided by love.

12 March

NEVER FORGET THE simplicity of meditation. Or, that simple isn't easy. It is easier if you start young and the older you are, the more you may have to unlearn. But it can also mean you have learned better what letting go means. It is so important, I think, to introduce contemplative practice, in prayer, as early as possible in life. Because it is part of our tradition of prayer, why not teach it at the outset of the journey of faith?

13 March

LEARNING TO LOVE others means to accept and see them for who they really are as themselves. We cannot do this if we are forcing them into the mould of our desires or fears or projecting our scripts onto them. Seeing all our relationships as sacraments of the divine reality brings us together into the centre where we all 'share in the very being of God' (2 Peter 1.4).

14 March

STILLNESS TRIGGERS THE withdrawal of projections. To love ourselves requires being still, letting go of self-imaging. To love others demands the same detachment. It happens because, even without knowing it at first, we are learning to be loved by God in the same stillness. Love for others and love for God are twin births of God's love for us. *We love because God loved us first* (1 John 4.10, 19).

15 March

THE EGO NOTICES our hunger for love but wants to be in control. It wants to be loved exclusively. It wants to woo and win God because it wants to be in charge. We need to move beyond our egocentricity that makes us imagine we love God before God loves us, or even loving God so that he *will* love us. The ego is tricky and complicates everything. It tries to control even God through its image of God. Recentre yourself in the centre of reality, that God loves us first. That experience of being loved impels a response in us that has no ego in it. God's love for us bounces back to him from us and we awaken to who we truly are.

16 March

MANY PEOPLE TODAY feel chronically lonely and desperately alienated. They long for intimate relationships but feel incapable of them. Online dating is a technological response to this that has some good results. It has the element of chance that village hall dances used to have before discos. Not having tried it I can't judge. But it seems to me the danger of computerising and classifying our desires may misrepresent and isolate them. Can algorithms turn fantasy into reality? As I have learned from some people who have tried, it can make them even more lonely. But, if God is everywhere, he's in algorithms too ... Nevertheless, I feel wary of technology occupying sacred ground. I may easily be wrong on this.

17 March

THE LETTER TO the Hebrews says that the Word of God is alive and active and sharper than a two-edged sword (4.12). This is a disturbing image if we think of it as a weapon or remember cutting ourselves with a sharp knife. But the same Word is also smooth, slipping through the confusions of our mind, reaching the core of truth in us. It re-humanises us and revives the process that makes for wholeness and communion. St Benedict, like others whose mind is permeated with Scripture, knew this effect of the Word. So, he urges us to learn the art of reading sacred words so that we in turn can be read into more intense life by the Word.

18 March

THE LOVE, THE joy, the peace, the patience, the kindness, the goodness, the fidelity – the 'fruits of the Spirit' – are not of our making. They are under our willpower. They are the manifestation, the evolution, the growing of seeds in our nature which are pre-existing potencies of the divine life and vivid signs of the Spirit. They are proof of the process of divinisation. God became human so that we might become God. Exactly what life is about.

19 March

PURE PRAYER IS the most wonderful and effective means available – as pure gift – to help us to stop identifying ourselves with the ego. It is our escape from Hell and release from the horror of being in prison. As prayer recentres us from the ego-zone to our true self, our entire personality resets. Appearances may remain the same but, interiorly, transformation is at work. We become the person we truly are and the person we are called to be. The truth of us surfaces, the false dissolves. A self-awareness begins revealing that we are a temple of God and that as a mature child of God we have found our primal relationship.

JESUS USES IMAGES of growth in his teaching parables to describe the experience of the Kingdom. St Irenaeus says famously, 'The glory of God is the human being fully alive.' In nature, life peaks through growth. Irenaeus expresses the aspiration to plenitude and implies the stages of development bringing us to that fullness. Glorifying God is not kowtowing to a superior being or paying homage. It is expanding our humanity, as we mature until we become what we see. Irenaeus added to his famous phrase, '... and the life of the human being is the vision of God'.

21 *March*

THE GOSPEL GREEK word for 'peace' (*eirene*) comes from the verb 'to join'. It reflects the beautiful Hebrew word *shalom* (Arabic *salaam*) which means wholeness and harmony. The first step in peace-making is to be rejoined to ourselves and thus find the harmonious wholeness of our true nature. No peace with others or our environment can endure if it is not connected to this inner peace with ourselves.

TIME DOES NOT heal by itself. If we feel forgiveness is blocked, even years after we were hurt – it is because we are stuck. We have not been levered into another level of consciousness. Unless we re-integrate the *negative other*, the enemy we have constructed, we cannot know God as the ultimate, all-inclusive other. We cannot be other-centred. We make a false god out of the fragments of our ego's fears, guilts, hurts and desires. Many people worship such false gods and actually hate the true God. It is false religion. A gulf of in-authenticity can open in religious people just because they will not give time *to be* with the living God. This God will not use force. But he never stops trying to get past the locked doors of our psyche and simply shoo away the little ego-god who is our idol and our gaoler.

23 *March*

JOHN MAIN SAYS the times of meditation are 'the most important times of the day'. If so, why? It doesn't make sense to us at first, or maybe for years. We need to have reached the point of seeing how and why meditation is a gift that has slipped into our life, is becoming part of us and that without it we feel incomplete. The day the meditator doesn't meditate, they miss something as important as food or sleep. They feel unbalanced, not guilty. It is not a matter of willpower. It is more like accepting a gift. In time practice brings us to that sense of gratitude that touches everything every day.

24 *March*

THE WAY OF self-knowledge is inherently therapeutic: it is a self-healing, a *oneing*, a way of being known. As I come to know myself, I am relaxing my defences and security systems and allowing myself to *be known*. To know that I am known is a higher level of knowledge: it means I am no longer fixated on myself. I am not reflecting on myself. I am reflected back to myself by others I know. So then, on a pathway of self-knowledge I risk myself by becoming open to others and to the never-failing wondrous beauty of the otherness of the cosmos.

25 March

WE ARE PART of a bigger story in ways we can partially see but never fully understand. Are we a self-contained subplot in the Big Story? Maybe this is not the best way to see ourselves: each and every human being, like each subatomic particle or wave, is uniquely necessary to complete the jigsaw of the whole cosmos. If at the end of time there was one piece missing from the jigsaw, creation would have to be replayed from the beginning. Maybe that's why history seems to repeat itself. There may only be a small bit of blue sky that's missing from the jigsaw but the completeness depends on it. Human value does not depend on size but uniqueness.

26 March

AS A MONK I have come to understand the contemplative life by seeing that it does not have to be lived in a monastery. In fact, you can live happily in a lovely monastery and still not live a contemplative life. Over the years and across continents, I have met more people living in the world, working, struggling and raising families who do live contemplatively. Travel has taught me stability and a global community has taught me solitude. (I am thankful to my abbot for allowing me to do this work.) Contemplative life is more than a quiet life, though environment and routine help. It is essentially about service, which helps take the attention off yourself in the regular times of contemplative practice. Each day attempting to live true to the true self, learning from failures and dying to the ego in trying to do what we have to do, that *is* the contemplative life. Love, change and joy witness to it. I like the monastic life (although most monasteries don't give monks much time to meditate); but every person can be true to themselves while making the world their monastery and their heart their monastic cell. A faithful meditator is also a true monk.

27 March

WE ARE EACH a singular manifestation of the divine. St Augustine's teaching on the Trinity is about how human nature itself is constructed as a microcosm of creation as a living, breathing icon of God. Sparks of God. The mystery of God is the boundless abyss of being and the eternal, loving mystery of the self. When the Word becomes flesh, it makes the invisible visible and the boundless measurable.

28 March

A KEY COMPONENT OF all spiritual discipleship is non-violence. To aspire to it seriously characterises the Christian life. There's no escaping it: the teaching of Jesus is to turn the other cheek, to love our enemies, to bless those who curse us. This is not the way of the world. It isn't the way politics or business operates. Revenge and retaliation are the normal responses to being attacked. To make the question more subtle, there are times when, collectively, we have a duty to defend ourselves in order to defend others. I have just returned from Ukraine and I felt, paradoxically, that their self-defence is an obligation, but I also saw the immense difference between the violence of the aggressor and that of the victim. The Christian disciple, like Arjuna in the Bhagavad Gita, must live with this paradox without denying Jesus' teaching. Daily meditation helps in war, perhaps is even necessary to hold this tension.

29 March

WE BEGIN BY repeating the mantra silently in our mind and heart. Saying it gently, attentively, lovingly and faithfully. Of course we become distracted from this simple task many, many, many times each meditation. That doesn't matter. We're earthen vessels containing the treasure of pure consciousness. We don't have to be perfect meditators or perfect disciples. What a liberation to know you don't have to be perfect. Just faithful. Keep returning to the mantra each time.

30 March

TRUE HOLINESS IS 'secret', meaning it's mysterious, un-self-conscious, more obvious to others than to one-self. Anyone who secretly thinks they are better or higher than others, despite the constant small victories of the ego, has hardly begun. For this reason, John Main said not to desire holiness. The deeper your practice, the less you will even think about perfection or spiritual achievement. We renounce the desire for holiness to discover the fact that we *are* holy. That is called humility or self-knowledge.

THE MOST REVOLUTIONARY process in life is self-knowledge, awakening to ourselves as we truly are. To cut through the ego's illusions and images, to cut through what we want other people to think about us, and just to be ourselves: that's the greatest transformation. It is the essential revolution of the gospel. To come to self-knowledge is the personal revolution, the metanoia, of the whole gospel vision of life. But, when it is genuine and sustained, it not only changes us. It changes the world that we belong to, beginning with the tiny microcosm of the cosmos where we live and work every day.

April

THE PURPOSE OF a true contemplative practice, like daily meditation, is to take the attention off ourselves. The practitioner is not observing or measuring what's happening. Mary, our right brain, our contemplative side, is taking over and supports Martha, our active side. This feels odd or uncomfortable at first, which is why it is called the way of unknowing: because we don't know where it is going to take us. It may feel disembodied, disorienting at first and that is a good sign. But meditate with children and you quickly see how whole, grounded and simple it is. The wonderful quality of a child that allows them to meditate so easily is their inherent holiness.

2 April

IN ANY SOCIAL group – even when its members have much in common or are even related by blood – each person is utterly unique. Amazingly so, just as every snowflake or crystal is unique. What does that reveal about the immense playfulness of the divine imagination? All we need to do about it is to *be* our uniqueness and value the uniqueness of others. Why do we imitate others? Why do we like to be absorbed in crowds? Is it because we are afraid of all uniqueness, including our own? The true saints and heroes took the risk to be themselves and became beacons of hope and inspiration for every social group.

HOW MANY 'PERFECT' lives have there been? Even the official 'saints' were far from perfect. Our heroes, like Gandhi, Martin Luther King and Nelson Mandela, had flaws and weaknesses. Is your spouse perfect? The Pope, who can sign a paper and 'make' a saint in the Catholic Church, said that even in their writings many saints got it wrong. Their saintliness was their acceptance of the overwhelming experience of being loved and of the goodness of human nature. They wanted to live and witness to this and bring others to that same awareness. They spun away from egotism towards the well-being of others. Seek perfection and approval and you become fake. Be open to the experience of love and you will be holy where it matters: for others, not for yourself.

I LIKE A STORY of Gandhi from his student days at Oxford. He had been reading the Gospel and felt powerfully drawn towards Jesus. Walking one day, he came across a beautiful little village church and decided to go in to pray. As he was opening the door, the vicar appeared. With a hostile look he asked Gandhi, 'Are you a Christian?' Gandhi said, 'No, sir, I am not but I would like to pray here.' The vicar told him he could not enter. What if this poor little defensive Christian had said, 'Welcome, this is the house of God for all peoples. Come in.'

CONTEMPLATION IS THE key we need to recover in modern Christianity. Maybe we didn't lose the key entirely but we certainly mislaid it. We locked ourselves out of our own house as a result. It is the key to the 'inner room' that Jesus tells us we must enter (Matt. 6.6) because contemplation is (as official theology claims) the goal of all prayer. It is also the heart, which the same official theology says 'develops a contemplative orientation in the people'. There is an essentially mystical dimension to Christian liturgy, especially the Eucharist, which in most cases has been lost. The same key opens the door to prophetic social action by treating the poor and marginalised as our equals. No less is it the key to the wisdom demanded by the new ethical dilemmas we face in science and technology. This little key is like a code that opens a forgotten deposit account that can save humanity. It is explicit in the teaching of Jesus on prayer in the Sermon on the Mount.

6 April

MEDITATION IS THE catalyst for personal integration and wholeness: so, in the Christian tradition it is called the 'prayer of the heart'. The *heart* is a symbol, not only of interiority or feelings; it is a universal spiritual symbol of wholeness, authenticity and integration. In heart-consciousness, all aspects of ourselves find unity.

7 April

IF WE FOUND what we truly desire we would find ourselves. But joy is deeper even than desire. It is the wisdom found in all spiritual traditions through recorded time. Meditation does not destroy desire because life without desire would be just algorithms, sub-human. It transforms desire. It reconnects you with what you truly desire, which is what you are destined for. It sorts us out in the process, because confusion and illusion arise from not knowing (or believing) what it is we really want. In a radical way meditation straightens us out by simplifying us and putting us back in touch with our basic need, which is also our basic desire. When need and desire meet, joy springs up.

8 April

IN THE CHRISTIAN contemplative tradition, self-knowledge is the prelude to knowing God. When you begin a contemplative practice this knowledge is more important than what you may or may not believe about God. 'Be still and know that I am God.' In stillness, belief yields to pure faith. Let stillness loosen the ego's grip over how you know yourself and God appears. Self-knowledge and the knowledge of God are one and therefore this knowing is love. Like the father in the parable of the Prodigal Son, God can let go of us but he cannot reject or punish anything he has made and with whose beauty he has fallen in love.

9 April

ST PAUL'S TRANSFORMING insight is that wherever there is sin, grace abounds all the more. This is a landmark breakthrough in religious consciousness. The more sin, the more grace. What a different conception of the sinful human condition than the equation of punishment proposed before. Neither law nor punishment heals sin: only grace. What is grace? Grace is the giving of self between persons. Love without demands, pure attention without an object, mercy without measure.

10 April

HEALTH IS THE integrated experience of wholeness that incorporates even what seems like its opposite. Sickness, suffering and death seem like the opposites of health as generally thought. But accepting them (which doesn't mean you go looking for them) means moving beyond denial and anger. We move then into the integral realm, where opposites meet. From every perspective, medical, psychological and spiritual, this is part of the healing process. It will lead the sick person to an even greater degree of healing, wholeness and health than they knew before.

11 April

THE BIG IDEAS of health and salvation are intertwined. Salus was the Roman goddess of welfare, health and prosperity, safety and security. A salve came to mean a healing ointment absorbed by the skin. Italians meet each other with the greeting '*salve*'. The meditator welcomes the bringer of divine welfare and absorbs it daily.

12 April

DESPITE OUR NEGLECT of them, the world still contains powerful wisdom traditions which are transmissions of high consciousness through history and culture. The primary form of this transmission is through personal relationship followed by a series of relationships, teaching experiences and discipleship. Wisdom passes through the generations and its language evolves and other expressions are provided by the culture, as in technology. Yet no genuine experience of wisdom is ever outdated. Today, when we come across a wisdom transmission, we may not recognise it at first but later we realise it is just what we have been seeking. It feels as if this wisdom was also seeking us. The important thing is that we have met and should travel through life together.

13 April

I HAVE IMMENSELY VALUED and benefited from my personal meetings and dialogues with the Dalai Lama over many years. He has an extraordinary gift for friendship, no doubt because he is so at peace with himself and is free from competitiveness in the ordinary sense of wanting to win. He teaches Buddhist wisdom but is not recruiting for converts. He recommends people stay in their own tradition, to discover and learn its treasures. He is also curious and respectful about the wisdom in all traditions. He says that we are free to change our tradition but adds that it is better to grow where you are planted. (Many Christians left their roots because they failed to find a transmission of wisdom there.) The mainstream churches tend not to think of Christians taking over the world. Other forms of Christianity are highly intolerant of other faiths. A weak Christianity, of shallow spiritual depth, however, means a weaker world. That is why teaching meditation in the Christian tradition answers the missionary element in the gospel. It is good news. Without crude marketing or sense of superiority, every church can strengthen the faith everywhere by nurturing a local contemplative prayer group.

14 April

THE WORD 'FAITH' is often confused with the word 'belief'. But faith is more about relationship while belief is about how we understand relationship. Just as we speak about a faithful marriage or friendship, faith is relationship in which we endure through good and bad times. Joyful fruits of that endurance appear and are cause for celebration. To say to someone, 'I will be faithful to you for ... umm ... at least a week' won't do it. Just as planting a tree and expecting it to be fully-grown overnight is fanciful. Faith grows. It aspires to the condition of unconditionality: in sickness and health, for better or worse. Faith is *personal* commitment, a gift of self that releases hope and eventually, inevitably, love.

SELF-KNOWLEDGE IS WORTH more than the short-lived miracles of technology. It cannot be measured or reduced to mere self-awareness. Yet as part of the process of self-knowledge, to be aware of our psychological character is important. It is even one of the fruits of spiritual practice. In self-knowledge, we cross into the mystery of being, first our own being but then the ground of being itself.

16 April

MEDITATORS FROM EVERY tradition share a knowledge of the challenges and fruits involved in their practice. When they meet they intuitively recognise each other, knowing what discipline means and why they follow it. Their differences are not eradicated or ignored but deepen their friendship. This illustrates the human contemplative community we are called to develop. The fruits of meditation are universal. Compare, for example, the *Dhammapada*'s list of benefits from meditation with St Paul's 'harvest of the spirit' in his Letter to the Galatians – love, joy, peace, patience, kindness, goodness, fidelity, gentleness and self-control. No copyright on these.

THE CHANGES WE see occurring in us through meditation are signs of the flowering of divine life in us. They emerge and spread to all aspects of our life. We begin to experience, with sheer surprise, that the 'meaning of life' may truly be what Christians call *theosis*: the human is being divinised. It can 'share fully in the life of God'. This begins here and now where we are planted. Meaning does not come from answers or ideologies. It is connection. Our short life is preparing for full interconnection with God and God's playground, the cosmos.

IN STILLNESS COMES knowledge: *Be still and know that I am God*. In this kind of knowing we find that we cannot know God as we solve a mathematical problem. We can never know God as an object. Stillness also leads us first into self-knowledge where we know what it is to be known. The stillness of meditation is a discipline of daily wisdom practised by pausing from activity, doing, thinking, judging and self-analysis. Life is refreshed and set free through this kind of stillness.

DAILY MEDITATION TEACHES us many things, including to 'keep death constantly before our eyes'. St Benedict, with many wisdom traditions, recommends this. It means to fully face life's impermanence and the fact that we have no abiding city. The teachings of Jesus remind us to live in the present moment, not try to build false securities in the denial of death. If we can indeed face impermanence without despair, denial or rage but with confidence, humour and faith, we have been set free from our deepest fear.

LOVE IS THE supreme gift of the Spirit. Lennon and McCartney were right, love is all we need. St Paul, teaching about the gifts of the Spirit, says to pursue the 'higher gifts', the highest being love. Jesus encapsulates his whole teaching and his life in the single commandment to 'love one another'. Whoever loves knows God. *Not*, 'whoever loves God knows God'. But whoever loves knows God. Meditation is the daily workout of our capacity to love.

SPIRITUAL VISION EXTENDS further than that of the scientific method. It shows us what the deepest space telescope cannot, that in addition to the known forces of the universe (strong, weak, electromagnetic and gravity), there is the force of love, which is the creative source of the cosmos and the background radiation everywhere. Love pervades human consciousness, every atom, every relationship, every thought and action. In ways that science has yet to explore, love is the heart of all creation and evolution. It unites inner and outer dimensions: the world of personal, solitary awareness and the world of relationship and interaction. This love is discoverable in our own deepest core. It is the essence of consciousness. It is the secret that hides itself openly everywhere.

22 April

OUR CAPACITY FOR love develops throughout all stages of natural growth. We grow into maturity to realise our infinite capacity for love and to become the person that we are called to become. Like every process, human development is a journey. It is a labyrinth with many turns and apparent repetitions. But it is also a single narrow path. If you feel lost in the labyrinth, just keep walking and you find we cannot really be lost. Consciously walking the labyrinthine path is mirrored in the journey of meditation itself morning and evening. A full step forward involves both feet. Seeing this journey-within-a-journey teaches us patience and faithfulness, and enfolds us in wisdom.

IN A NEGATIVE spirituality we focus upon sinfulness. There may be a lot: jealousies, lusts, failures, pride, anger, violence and other not unhappy states. All such negative forces are a flow-back from a blocked ego. We come to a stagnant standstill in the congestion of fears and desires. In this state, God seems an irrelevant absurdity, even to some a super-parental tyrant always disapproving and punishing. Someone told me once, 'You know, nothing happens during my meditation. I plod along every day with only an occasional breakthrough moment. But now for the first time I understand what "God is love" means. I don't know how I understand it, but I know it's true. It's like the fog is clearing.'

24 *April*

'I DON'T KNOW what loving myself means.'
'Try becoming still.'
'What is stillness?'
'Stillness comes with a liberating discipline. It is the process of transcendence. The more still we are, the more the horizons move and we transcend our limitations.'
'What does that mean?'
'Stillness doesn't mean stopping. It is not static. We see it in the miracle of growth in all nature.'
'Yes, but ...'
'This relationship between stillness and growth is what you find in meditation.'
'I thought you'd say that.'
'Yes. Sorry.'

WE CANNOT BE still without learning how to love ourselves. The stillness of meditation is the best teacher
because it teaches through our own experience. We learn
to treat our own anger, judgementalism and intolerance
with compassion. Meditation is, in the first instance anyway, self-administered natural medicine with only beneficial
side-effects. It releases the force of self-healing through contact
with spirit. As we enter this school of love, we learn how love
of self leads to love of others and cascades into love of God.
All love is one love. There is one reality. We are in relationship
but solitude is necessary to reveal how. Especially when others
hurt or betray us (or we them). Solitude is necessary to stay
in love. Solitude is the first step we take as we sit in stillness.
Relationship follows it quickly.

TO LOVE OURSELVES helps us to live a life of spontaneous
gratitude for the gift of being. It is the best way I know
to understand the idea of 'praising God'. I don't think we
can praise God unless we have learned to love ourselves. Not
liking ourselves leads to hating God. Whatever pious picture
we have of God, if we cannot like ourselves, faults included,
we may really hate the God who made us and then express
it by the way we treat others. This may sound simplistic but
think about it. Silence, stillness, simplicity, the work of contemplative practice is not easy but it is worth it.

IN LOVING THOSE closest to us we withdraw even our
positive projections which are ways we idealise and idolise
them until the romantic spell wears off. In loving our enemies
we withdraw our negative projections, that is, the ways we
blame them to excuse or justify ourselves for what is going

wrong. Like scapegoating Jews for social conspiracy problems, or gays for destroying family values, or immigrants for badly run economies. We transfer onto them our anger, hurt and despair. Withdrawing all projected illusions is the first task of contemplative practice.

28 April

IN THE SOLITUDE of meditation we see how no one can take from us what is truly ours: our essential goodness is inalienable and it cannot be hacked as only God is the password. Our worst enemy, to whom we are most vulnerable, cannot do it. Forgiveness is not a pardon we bestow on others but a gift to ourselves to lay down the burden of enmity and free us from the constraints of victimhood. Forgiveness takes us deep into our wounded humanity. It is complete when, like Jesus, we understand those who hate us. We forgive as we come to know ourselves.

LOVE OF SELF, love of others. I'd like to ask you to think of the third aspect of love, the love of God. As our mind becomes more habitually contemplative, we see the gap between what we think of God and how we experience this reality for which no word suffices. Part of the challenge when religious people start the contemplative journey is the size of this gap. 'Mind the gap' is the recorded announcement of the wisdom of the London Underground. Be careful not to fall into the gap between the God beyond images and the God we imagine. It is, however, also the space that allows us to grow. It can feel quite resistant to being bridged at first because it is structural, like the distance between the train and the platform. But the incarnation of the Word has actually already bridged it.

WHAT COULD BE more obvious than that God loves us first? God manifests his love in creation. He loves what he creates and nothing exists that did not come out of his love. Existence is the visible expression of Being. Yet all the time we forget the obvious. God, not me, is the source and centre of reality. I am not. However much this may offend the ego, it is the truth discovered in the practice of meditation.

May

1 May

BY RECALLING THAT God loves us first and bowing before that obvious truth we enter the essential Christian experience: 'The love of God floods our inmost heart through the Holy Spirit he has given us.' We know ourselves loved because we exist and because beyond existence we can experience being. The best proof is experience, said Francis Bacon, the founder of the scientific method. This is the experience of meditation. Accepting this enables us to love ourselves, friends and foes and strangers and, in them, God.

2 May

THE EGO EVEN in a grown person is as self-absorbed as a child. It wants to love God first because it always sees itself as first and centre. As we grow beyond egocentricity it fights a rearguard action and tries to manipulate and control even God. But faith recentres in the true centre of reality. Here we accept the reality that God loves first and the experience of being loved bestows on us the wisdom of humility. All this may not take a religious expression but it is what salvation, liberation, enlightenment mean.

3 May

THE LAST FEW days' readings have been attempting to say: 'God is love, and whoever dwells in love is dwelling in God and God in them. This is for us the perfection of love: to have confidence on the Day of Judgement. And this we can have because, even in this world, we are as he is. There is no room for fear in love. Perfect love banishes fear, for fear brings with it the pains of judgement, and anyone who is afraid has not attained to love in its perfection. We love because he loved us first' (1 John 4.16–19).

4 May

WE ARE THE image of God, and this image of God is made visible in Jesus, who reflects to us who we truly are. He is the mirror, as it were, of our true self, the image of the invisible God. Meditation is constantly teaching us that we must let go of God, the God of our minds, the God of our concepts, in order to love God. This is the same lesson we also learn through all human relationships. To love, we must let go: we must move beyond the image of the other person that has formed in our minds in order to find the reality. No relationship can be authentic and enduring unless we move beyond the image to the reality – unless we let go of the person we love. We cannot know union without renunciation.

5 May

COMPUNCTION OF HEART is central to the Desert Teachers' wisdom. It refers to the breaking-open of the heart-centre and is sometimes accompanied by actual tears. Some people even frequently experience this 'gift of tears'. Sometimes they think they are a bit odd and say 'I'm meditating and suddenly I find myself crying all the way through it, not sobbing but a steady flow of tears.' The Desert Mothers and Fathers understood this as a grace and prayed for the gift of tears! Not all tears are wet. Cassian says, compunction of heart accompanied by the gift of tears leads to pure joy, a release and relief from repression that frees you from the cares and anxieties about 'fleshly things'. This is not escapism, just proof that you can really lay aside problems during the time of meditation. Cassian says, don't force it. As John Main, a modern Desert Father, says about meditation: just do it, be faithful to the twice-daily meditation and the natural process will follow. This is reassuring but also challenging: he also said that a twice-a-day practice is a minimum although it takes time and patience to build it.

6 May

TO SAY SOMETHING I often hear, 'I'm not a good meditator', betrays (I think) that you want to be (or think you should be) a perfect meditator. People also often say disparagingly, 'I lead a weekly meditation group – but it's very small.' They might mean a group with about ten or twelve members faithful over many years and always open to new people, and I tell them many groups are smaller than that. Faith, not size, matters. Jesus said, 'Where two or three are gathered in my name, I am there.' It is strange that we forget this and remain so concerned just about numbers. A true spiritual group will be realistic about material issues but should have foremost in their mind that authenticity is more important than popularity or success. 'Who is more feeble than a Christian?' Cassian asks. 'What is weaker than a monk?' That is the attitude that develops the beatitude of poverty of spirit.

JOHN MAIN MADE an important contribution to the Christian contemplative tradition by his teaching on the mantra which continued but evolved the teaching. In the fifth century, Cassian taught monks to say the word *continuously* throughout all activities (even while asleep). John Main addressing a modern lay audience put the emphasis on a (minimum) twice-daily practice of 20 to 30 minutes. If you do this, he taught, you will find that a degree of the 'continuous prayer' envisaged by Cassian will grow. The mantra moves from head to heart, sounding more subtly as we listen to it with purer attention. At first you *say* it 'in your head', constantly distracted. But gradually it sinks into heart-consciousness where the mantra begins to *sound*. Then we come to *listen* to it as our attention becomes single-pointed. In God's own time, it may lead us into 'pure prayer', which Cassian also calls the 'prayer of fire'. Purity means being 'nothing but what you are'. By this stage of the journey, the fire of the Spirit has purified us and led to union beyond divided consciousness.

WHAT SHOULD WE do when our attention is badly distracted? Keep dropping the thoughts. Just drop the distraction and return to the work of attention. But gently, humbly, don't try too hard. Come back to the single point. Humbly come home and start repeating it again. It is helpful to stay with the same word all the way through the meditation period and from day to day. Don't keep moving to another home. Coming back to the word is a blessed stability. It contains the miracle of faith.

BREATHING. VERY IMPORTANT. Keep breathing. Don't divide your attention between saying the word and using a breath technique. Let the wheel of the breath lightly support the mantra. The work is to keep returning to your mantra. Say your word faithfully and gently and let it guide the mind into the heart. The entrance to the heart has a low door, like the Church of the Nativity in Bethlehem. That was designed so that everyone – kings, paupers, geniuses, the forgotten and despised, the high and mighty – had to bow low to enter the sacred place of the Birth.

EVEN THOUGH MEDITATION is simply laying aside your thoughts, mental activity continues to flow like motorway traffic, sometimes heavy, sometimes congested, sometimes fast-moving. Obsessive thoughts that keep returning to plague you or flashes of insight that delight and amaze, let go of them all. Everyone has certain emotional thought loops that play over and over. The best way to interrupt them is to return to the mantra. Meditation does not solve every problem. But it shows us a radical new way of handling them. A way called peace.

11 May

STATES OF CONSCIOUSNESS are ever-changing and can be changed. You may sit down to meditate brim-full of anxiety, stress, fear or distraction and, at the end of the meditation, you may stand up peace-filled, clear and calm. You may then say, 'What was all that fuss about? I can handle this; and if I can't, if there's nothing I can do, why fret?' Meditation has this capacity to calm the mind. But it takes practice.

12 May

UNDERSTANDING THE SIMPLICITY of meditation begins with posture, the way we sit. Meditation is not an abstract or merely cerebral experience, although when you begin it may seem as if you are entirely in your head. Most of us are so much in our thoughts and fantasies that we feel the confusion of this most of the time. But if you meditate, you find that you move, as it were, from head to heart. Everything we are is in the heart – our body, mind, feelings, joys and griefs – as the point of wholeness and the work of integration. A good sitting posture reflects the still point of the heart. It is balanced, relaxed and alert, neither slouching nor rigid. The head is poised on top of the torso and the shoulders and feet hold our equilibrium. If the posture is good, you can meditate better and for longer in comfortable, still uprightness.

13 May

THE PORTAL OF paradox opens into the mystery of reality. Discovering who you uniquely are is part of this openness to the real in the present moment. Knowing it, you must relate to others in a freer and wiser way. The fruits of meditation soon manifest at the level of all your relationships. Progress on the contemplative path is not about levitating, developing psychic powers or accessing any kind of 'supernatural' realm of existence. Reality and nature are one.

Entering into the real through the portal of paradox involves taking the attention off ourselves. Jesus said that it is more difficult for a rich man to enter the Kingdom than for a camel loaded with merchandise to pass through the eye of a needle. We need to slim down and travel light on this path. We waste a lot of time in the ego's loop of thought, analysing and solving our problems, repeating stress-related situations, anxious about deadlines, complicated relationships, worrying about happiness, financial or medical problems. All this is extra baggage that keeps our attention on ourselves. Leave it all behind at the time of meditation and you'll slip through the eye of the needle surprisingly well.

15 May

LET YOUR MIND be remade. Adapt yourself no longer to the patterns set by this world: metanoia. Meditation is a practice that distils universal wisdom. If you are doing it authentically, faithfully, you are undergoing metanoia. At times it is hard work. Sometimes it is effortless. But it is always good work. The mantra is the little lever that lifts the burden of the ego off ourselves.

16 May

THE WORK OF silence takes us to three different but connected levels. We come to them in the time-frame of the spirit not our own. Contemplation is always gift, not the automatic result of a human technique. First, there is the silence of the tongue, the silence of the stillness of the body. Next, the silence of the mind, the stilling and leaving behind of thought and imagination. Eventually, there is the silence of the spirit itself which contains the fullest possible communication in a communion of love. Body, mind, spirit: distinct but interweaving levels or spheres on the scale of silence. In the process we bounce up and down the scale quite a lot. The spiritual journey is process but not linear progress. But we do need to tick off certain stages we need to cover. For example, if we can't control our tongue, there is not much hope for controlling our mind. And the silence of the mind has many subtle levels before it reaches the silence of the spirit.

17 May

I LOVE RAMANA MAHARSHI'S saying, 'The sparkling of truth devoid of "I" is the greatest austerity.' The greatest of Indian sages, who died in 1952, underwent an experience of unified consciousness at the age of 16. Ten years later he spoke for the first time from the non-dual silence he was plunged into. Visitors came to him from every part of the world. He did not 'take' disciples. Nor did he get involved in the ashram that grew around him except to ensure the guests were cared for properly. He taught mostly through silence and his loving gaze. Ramana's teaching revolved around the sun of 'self-enquiry'. He showed that the experience of Being is timeless, transcultural, transhistorical, as Moses also discovered on Mount Sinai. It is blindingly, obviously manifest in great teachers. Like Ramana, they insist as Jesus did that the Kingdom is within us (and among us). Only pierce through the layers of illusion and denial to the source of the I-thought where the Self manifests. Then, in whatever kind of life it is your destiny to find yourself, the truth sparkles without the ego's filtering distortion.

18 May

SILENCE IS THE most effective language to commune with the experience Ramana describes. John Main said that words and self-consciousness must go if full consciousness is to dawn. We should not try to experience the experience, anticipate it, imagine it or think about it. Be one with it. To be one is to be. Silence introduces us to being simple, not through words or concepts, which are self-referring. You don't know what a word means so you look it up in a dictionary; that definition doesn't help much either, so you look up those words and go round and round in circles. Silence breaks that circularity of words and delivers us to the open centre of the labyrinth of language.

19 May

THERE IS NO gift worth accepting more than the gift of Being, the basis of everything. Our own being is God's gift of himself, because God is Being. We, like everything else, share in the being of God. It is not a gift given for a limited lifespan. It flows forever like a stream or the ocean which the stream seeks and flows into.

20 May

THE WORK OF the mantra is demanding. It is like going to the gym (which I have tried and gave up on). It is real exercise, which is the meaning of the word 'ascesis'. We notice our mind becomes more agile just as after physical exercise we feel the body is healthier. Clarity of mind is developed by the muscle of attention which we work on in meditation and which will then work better during the rest of the day. We will notice how life is enhanced by being more aware, more attentive to people, to the environment and also to changes in our structures of consciousness. Because of this wide influence, meditation moves to the centre of life although it occupies only a small part of our time. It sheds light on the meaning of all experience through the expansion of attention and the intensification of love that results.

21 May

OVER TIME WE become better at handling distractions and we make lifestyle changes which harmonise the inner and the outer and so we become less distracted. Even in distraction, however, the healing process continues. We always need healing. Some wounds are deep, like St Paul's thorn in the flesh that we may be stuck with for life. While we are in the physical body, the ego is also going to be with us and the ego easily becomes a troublemaker. As contemplative consciousness expands, earlier stages of development are not left behind but integrated into the experience of wholeness and unity.

22 May

IN MANY ASIAN traditions meditation is practised through attention to the breath. In the Christian tradition of Orthodox and Latin Churches, the practice that leads to the heart has characteristically been the prayer-word: saying the word, listening to the mantra (of course while breathing). Asian traditions also honour the mantra as a primary method. Clearly there is no polarisation and many meditators who follow the mantra integrate it with the breath while keeping the primary focus on the word. For the Christian in the biblical tradition, the mantra evolves in the theology of the Word of God, at the Creation, then through the Prophets, culminating in the Incarnation. In meditation in Christian faith, then, we can say we share in the continuous creation of the world; we receive the 'word of the Lord' today as the Hebrew prophets did; and, like Mary we allow the Word to become our own flesh. 'Let it be done unto me, according to your word.' In the meditator, the Word becomes flesh as the mantra roots in the heart and releases the ever-present origin in whom we live and move and have our being.

DAILY PRACTICE OF meditation sensitises us to the 'interior senses'. This is an ancient notion that we come to experience in subtle but real ways. We 'feel' when we are going through a period of *acedia* – discouragement, boredom or depression. Once felt it can be better accepted. Whether it is a light or strong acedia, we traverse it better by consciously feeling it. If we need help, we can seek it. The sense of acedia reminds us it won't last for ever. As it passes we transition to a sense of a fresh and deeper state of *apatheia* – the health and harmony of the soul. With experience our interior senses help to recognise what we are passing through and keep us on the path.

THE TRUTH – NO false humility – is meditators are always beginners, never experts. 'Do not desire to be called holy until you are really holy,' St Benedict says. We can be happy that we have developed a practice but never take it for granted. Pride always has a fall, as the Desert Teachers reminded their disciples. The first step is always present and it is always the next step. That is grounded humility and gives a taste of wisdom. Progress is hidden in faithful repetition. In monastic life and for everyone with a contemplative practice there is a core element of repetition, a cyclical rhythm. But what is repeated is never exactly the same: the wheel of prayer turns faithfully not mechanically. The sign of this distinction is that systemic change – metanoia – is happening.

25 May

ACHIEVING CONTINUOUS PRAYER needs regular practice and external encouragement. The psycho-spiritual dynamic of community offers the encouragement needed to renew the freshness of engaging with our calling and commitment, whether monastic or marital. Without human encouragement, I think it is too hard, except for one in a hundred million, to make this journey seriously, wholeheartedly and joyfully. If we are truly committed, it is because we have felt the call to continuous prayer lifting us free from the ego. Staying open to encouragement from others, we widen the doors of our tent to the transmission of wisdom. Then we understand the source from which the encouragement of others reaches us.

26 May

THE WORK OF the mantra is to bring the mind to stillness: to take the searchlight of attention off ourselves. Maybe hard but what a relief and liberation! Every ascetical practice is a boost to moderation and deeper enjoyment, whether in eating, sleeping, sexual life or learning. It can be taken to extremes by the ego but the test of good ascesis is gentleness, no compromise but no violence against ourselves. If we use force, we turn the ascesis into a technique managed under the ego's control. How can the ego transcend egotism? Therefore, the ascesis of meditation must itself be egoless, a gentle way of letting go of control while committing to a discipline. To follow this regularly (on a daily basis) makes for a spiritual path. It soon teaches the mysteries and signs of the Spirit.

THE SPIRITUAL DIMENSION cannot be measured. We measure most things: how much a factory produces; how our weight or blood pressure is doing, our progress in a language, even the amount of our religious practice. But the spiritual, by its nature, disables the tools of measurement. Jesus said that the Spirit is like the wind. It comes from where we do not know, and it goes we know not where. But we feel it on our skins or when it blows a cap off our head, we see its effects. The wind in the trees or over water may be terrifyingly strong or comfortingly gentle but we cannot control it. Nor can we measure progress on this daily path; but we can feel and sense it.

JOHN CASSIAN DESCRIBES the mantra as a 'fixed mark' upon which the mind focuses to come to stillness. This image reminds me of Shakespeare's Sonnet 116:

> Love is not love
> Which alters when it alteration finds,
> Or bends with the remover to remove.
> O no, it is an ever-fixèd mark
> That looks on tempests and is never shaken;
> It is the star to every wand'ring bark
> Whose worth's unknown, although his height be taken.

The Cloud of Unknowing describes the mantra as a 'dart' with which we 'beat upon the cloud of unknowing'. The Upanishads describe it as a bow that shoots the arrow of the self into the heart of God. John Main describes it as a plough passing over a rough field, a harmonising sound, a radio signal on the frequency of the Mind of Christ like a radar signal leading a plane in to land through fog.

CASSIAN WARNS OF two great dangers in prayer: the *sopor letalis*, the lethal sleep, and the *pax perniciosa*, the pernicious peace, which is drowsiness rather than wakefulness. John Main called it like being 'piously stoned', numbed and dumbed in half-sleep. Fidelity to the mantra helps us over these dangers. Cassian sees it uniting all levels of consciousness, bringing us to unity and vision. It embraces everything we can think or feel. Neither Cassian nor Main sees this as rejection or suppression but as integration. Both see this prayer of radical simplicity and poverty as a way to union.

30 May

FOR CASSIAN THE 'formula' or mantra grows out of immersion in Scripture and becomes rooted in the heart by practice. By the 'constant repetition' and 'revolution' of this verse in the heart, he says, it roots itself deeply and so continuously in consciousness. He says, you will fall off to sleep repeating this verse and you will wake in the morning repeating it. When you are working or answering the call of nature. It is the prayer of the heart that never sleeps. 'I sleep but my heart is awake,' says the Song of Songs. It is pure prayer. It embodies the theology of prayer and the goal of a Christ-centred life, to be one in body, mind and spirit with the One who is one: with the Mind of Christ in every human heart.

31 May

MEDITATION IS THE lived theology of the simple practice of pure prayer that Cassian and John Main and the hesychast tradition recommend. A way of radical simplicity. The Latin word *simplex* was a tailoring term referring to how a piece of cloth was (un)folded. Folded, it is duplex or complex. Pure prayer unfolds and simplifies both mind and heart. When consciousness is merely self-conscious, reflecting on itself, we become over-complex, endlessly duplicating ourselves.

June

BECOMING MORE FULLY, more freely alive is a benefit of self-knowledge. It develops through the silence of the daily times of meditation. Finding one's true self cannot be a self-centred activity. It is always to find ourselves essentially *other-centred*: turned towards others and the ultimate otherness (to which we give the name 'God') and who is so other-centred that it gives us back to ourselves after it has absorbed us. Other-centredness is not a concept or ideal because it is concerned about others, caring and compassionate towards their suffering. Nor is it a choice we make but a truth of our own nature we discover. When we think of ourselves as egocentric, we surprise ourselves by acting otherwise. Something shifted in us (metanoia) showing us that who we are is inseparable from who we are *with*.

WE YEARN TO find ourselves. We also need to understand that it only happens if we are prepared to lose ourselves. The need to find our true self is the driving force in human development. At every stage of life's journey – physical development, psychological, sexual, emotional – it is the inescapable push and pull from within. It restores us when we are defeated and it makes all success feel incomplete. We are never satisfied for long even when we get what we want. We always feel 'there's more'. And there is.

3 June

J ESUS' TEACHING ON finding oneself doesn't present it as a something we find but identifies it with *following* him. This is a different spin on it. What does 'follow' mean? Say you and a friend are driving somewhere in two cars. He knows the way, you don't. So, he says, 'Just follow me.' What does that mean? It means trust that, 'I know where I am going.' To follow a trusted friend who knows the way means they are the way for you. But you will need to pay attention to them or you may get lost. This is the spirit of faith.

4 June

T HERE ARE TWO sides to the coin of finding oneself: losing oneself and finding that *we are found*. Discovering that we are found is more expansive, it happens in a bigger space than anything we could call 'myself'. It involves another. The whole idea of 'self' changes when self-knowledge dawns. This is an insight into human consciousness, found in the gospel teaching, of great urgency for our time. We have sunk so far into a culture of narcissism and so conditioned by a training in self-fixation. It is an individualism and self-important entitlement linked cruelly at the same time to loneliness and low self-esteem.

5 June

W E CANNOT SEEK ourselves as separate from ourselves. When we come close to our self, it is much simpler than it sounds. It is not finding something new but recognising who we are. We don't acquire anything; we shed much unnecessary baggage. Anxiety, self-division and the chronic feeling of separation and duality all diminish. The perceived distance between us, the world and God shrinks, eventually to nothing. At the end of his life, Buddha was asked, 'What did you get out of meditation?' He replied, 'Nothing.' People were shocked. 'But,' he added, 'I lost a lot.' This is what Jesus means by linking true happiness to poverty of spirit.

SILENCE IS NEEDED for selfhood to emerge out of the chaos of the ego: from the history of pain, loss and fantasy, of lopped memories, the dense jungle of the mind. The older we get, the thicker the jungle, until we see a way through it, the narrow path of contemplation that leads to life. Before we even begin to appreciate what 'true self' means, we need to find this path of silence which clears the jungle and even expands the spaciousness we travel in.

TRUE SILENCE IS a power to be reckoned with. There's a look-alike, false silence ('I'm never going to speak to her again' or 'Please don't speak to me'). It is cancelling rather than working through. There is also a negative, untruthful silence of brushing something under the carpet in case people get upset, or suppressing it because we feel threatened by transparency. In true silence, however, we experience liberation from fear, expansion of mind and opening of the heart in a new degree of communication arising from communion with others. The test of true silence is that it brings us peace with ourselves and with others.

THINK HOW MANY times you have made mistakes – mis-judging people, mishandling situations, over-estimating your capacity. The ego is usually party to our big mistakes. But when ego subsides and eventually disappears (temporarily) like a puff of smoke, then the constructions and justifications of the false self disappear with it. This dethroning of the ego is the result of renunciation. We don't renounce the good things in life, only our attachment to them. What we renounce is anything false. Attachment reduces our capacity even to see the good things. Silence is the work of renunciation. The false things and our attachment to them keep up endless chatter until they meet silence.

IN CHRISTIAN UNDERSTANDING, self-knowledge arises from the pure point of union with the Risen Christ, that point at which he and I are 'one undivided person'. So, if he and you are one, what does that imply about my relationship with others? If each person is in the same undivided union with Christ that I am, does it not follow that each of us forms 'one undivided person' with each other? I look at you, you look at me across the divide: we disagree on many things; we agree a little; you like me, I like you, you don't like me, I don't like you. At these levels differences matter and obscure our oneness. But at the ground level, you and I are one in union with Christ.

IT IS WISE to always be aware of how much we don't know. This not only keeps us humble but also frees up space to grow into the higher level of knowledge where we know because we are known. St Paul says: 'Now we see through a glass darkly, but then we will see face to face. Now I know in

part, but then I shall know even as I have been fully known'
(1 Cor. 13.12).

11 June

A CONTEMPLATIVE PRACTICE HELPS bring us to what
mystical thinkers have called the first stage of contemplation: the 'contemplation of nature'. This means being
consciously present to the world around you. This being
present is not just observing or objectifying but knowing that
you are, belong to and participate in the world. Then a sym-
bolic perception arises in which we see the universe's system
of signs and wonders. Seeing is connecting and connecting is
seeing the meaning of the world in its order and beauty. Deeper
practice leads to the same awareness of our inner environment.
Here we recognise mental and behavioural patterns and may
say, 'Well, that's part of me; it's causing me trouble or even
shames me but there is beauty here too and order.'

12 June

TO BE AWAKE involves more than psychological awareness of one's history and patterns of behaviour. This will
come to light naturally with the multi-level work of contemplation. Self-knowledge consists of many stages. First, it is
experiencing the simple fact of existence, unconditional being,
that is greater than me or any individual identity. From this
experience of being we come to know that we belong. We
sense we are growing into and as part of a reality that transcends my single 'me' and my individual existence. We will be
remembered at our funeral as an individual and maybe will be
painfully missed by those who loved us. Let's hope they also
saw the greater reality that we and they belong to and whose
life is greater than death.

IN CHRISTIAN WISDOM, God is a trinity. It is a communion, a community of love. This communion is Being, not a being but Being itself. The 'ground of Being', as the mystics call it. It is not a platonic perfection or mathematical abstraction. It is love as we can only begin to understand it through the multiple expression of human love and our need for love. God is a cascading, overflowing, personal energy of love. How can we ever know this unimaginable God? By loving each other to our best capacity. This allows God to create – to reproduce – in us as holograms of God's self. The human is so much in the image of God that we are capable of Being as we become one with our source. Life is a school of love.

'BE STILL AND know that I am God.' In stillness comes knowledge. In this we come not only to know God but to know ourselves 'for the first time'. The stillness of meditation leads into this as we stop doing, thinking, judging, planning, analysing and all the rest. As we learn to be still, knowledge of our spirit arises. In that spiritual intelligence we find ourselves on the path that takes us beyond ourselves. Each step frees us to live more free from filters, preconceptions and fear.

15 June

OUR CONCEPTS AND preconceptions, our prejudices and filters diminish the fullness of life we can enjoy. In meditation, radical simplicity – letting go for a moment of all conceptual frameworks – delivers us from the prison we have made for ourselves. We taste the (to us at first) *dizzying* freedom of God, the glorious liberty of the children of God. It is a discovery for which the word 'amazing' – causing us to be confused and in a state of wonder – feels right.

16 June

WHAT HAPPENS DURING the times of meditation is less significant than the influence it has over the whole of our life. It is a difficult truth to accept as we like memorable experiences rather than gradual transformation. At the beginning of the journey we especially want to be persuaded we are not wasting time. Maybe for this reason we can experience some memorable moments in the early days. Gradually we let go of demands and expectations. Our perception expands to see what is happening in the greater landscape of life. That is a new way of seeing. Perceiving the priority of love in everything, we ourselves become the fruit of the practice.

17 June

I LEARNED FROM JOHN MAIN to think of love as the real outcome of meditation. In order to mark your progress, then, see if your capacity to give and receive love in unexpected (not necessarily romantic) ways is changing. Ask yourself why love is said to be the central reality of life. This is proven by how we judge our life on our deathbed. There is no better reason to meditate.

18 June

JOHN MAIN THOUGHT, in a very positive way, that life is a preparation for the moment of death. What we are like when that approaches is of great importance. Daily meditation is a preparation for the day of our death, for that moment of total letting go. Our ego dies and with it our acquisitiveness, number oneness, fantasies and fears. Meditation prepares us for that moment of naked encounter with reality as an inescapable day of release. This is because we are learning to die in meditation and so we are learning to live. 'Keep death constantly before your eyes,' St Benedict advised in a Rule of Life designed to face the impermanence of life without denial.

19 June

THROUGH OUR DAILY dying to the ego we see the meaning of forgiveness. No one can take away from us what is truly and uniquely ours. Our goodness, our value, our true identity are inalienable. Even if we feel we have lost these qualities through abuse or rejection, we have not. Forgiveness is a process of recovering them. It takes us deep into our damaged, wounded state. From that perspective we see the universal woundedness of humanity, including all those who hurt us. Forgiveness is released when we see our own beauty again, which gives us the confidence to look at our enemies with compassion.

20 June

PITY IS LESS than compassion. It is what we experience when we feel for someone who is suffering but our empathy is woven into our fear. When, for example, we see a dying person our own fear of death is secretly activated. Under the influence of that fear, we are not yet com-passionate, *suffering with*, the dying person; we pity them. We unconsciously think, 'Thank God it's not me.' When love meets suffering free from the ego-dynamic of fear, we no longer think of the other as a 'poor thing'. We hardly 'think' of them at all – giving advice, recommendations, looking for comforting words. We see them in ourselves and ourselves in them. We are truly *with* them.

21 *June*

AUTHENTIC COMPASSION HAPPENS when we recognise others in ourselves and ourselves in them. We mourn with those who mourn, we die with those who die, we suffer with those who suffer. We dance with those who dance. This is Christ's full-spectrum compassion which unites all humanity: 'When you give a cup of water to a thirsty person, you give it to me. What you do to the least of my little ones, you do to me' (Mark 9.41).

THE TRUE LOVE of self that we learn in the stillness of meditation releases in us a power to love all other people. We do not need enemies so why do we imagine we have them? As we accept the relationships of our life as sacred ground, as sacraments, we learn the art of withdrawing all our projections from them. To love ourselves we must accept ourselves just as we are and find that what we find is loveable. To love others means refusing to allow them power over us through the projection of enmity.

COMMUNITIES, FAMILIES OR marriages do not exist just to satisfy the members of those groups. They exist for those outside the membership group as well. They radiate outwards, far beyond themselves. Think of the influence of a loving family, the spouses' love for each other and for their children and the love of brothers and sisters. The joy of that experience touches those outside the charmed circle, welcoming whoever comes into contact with it. That was John Main's vision of a community of love that first inspired me to become a monk. But what community or family is ever perfect? The vision and love of the good avoids perfectionism. Therefore, it stops the shadow image appearing – the xenophobic tribe, the abusive family, a social media of hate, the excluding community. These aberrations also have a far-reaching influence.

WE ONLY KNOW God by love. This is the teaching of the whole Christian transmission of wisdom. God cannot be contained in any thought or legal system, in any physical place or institution, in any race or tribe. Is there anything God cannot do? Yes, God cannot prevent himself from being known by love. We must unlearn all preconceptions of how to love God.

I was once with a woman who was dying. She was frequently tormented by the fear that she did not love God, despite being a good woman who had lived a good life. Nevertheless, she underwent this terrible anguish on her deathbed. She thought she did not love God. Slowly and painfully she came to understand (with the help of a quote from St Augustine that amazed her) that the desire to love God is itself the love of God.

25 June

ENLIGHTENMENT DAWNS AS ego sets. Fear and desire yield to the freedom to love those who believe differently from ourselves and even those who cause us suffering. The ultimate weapon of non-violence replaces tools for vengeance. The whole person is changed. We taste the universal in ourselves and surrender ourselves to God. The conflict of opposites becomes the experience of transcendence, which is not a momentary event, but unfolds in a new way and vision of life. It is all unobservable, but it can be recognised as soon as we allow ourselves to be known. We can see it in people of every faith. We can serve this vision even before it is fully realised in our individual selves because we are more than individuals. Our great traditions teach us that there are communions of saints and that we belong to them. That our greatest resources are not material or technological but spiritual. The great teachers and lovers of humanity endlessly work to heal the wounds of sin and division.

26 June

I WONDER WHAT ST John means when he says that, 'God is greater than our conscience' (1 John 3.20). It is a liberating statement which we only understand from God's angle. I think it means that God's knowledge of us is deeper than our self-understanding, stronger than our guilt, more powerful than our fear of punishment.

OPENING OUR OWN experience to the transmission of wisdom from enlightened minds, we learn that the only morality is the morality of love. Forgiveness or compassion are not signs of weakness because they are in the very structure of reality. Jesus said his father is equally loving to 'good and bad alike'. So everyone who loves *is* a child of God.

'GOD IS LOVE, and whoever dwells in love is dwelling in God and God in them. This is the perfection of love for us: to have confidence on the Day of Judgement. And this we can have because, even in this world, we are as he is. There is no room for fear in love. Perfect love banishes fear, for fear brings with it the pains of judgement, and anyone who is afraid has not attained to love in its perfection. We love because he loved us first' (1 John 4.16–19). This supremely confident statement needs no commentary apart from how we live it.

PEOPLE SOMETIMES OBJECT to meditation as transcending the ego because they think we should build up the ego
before we transcend it. First, the ego can be weak or strong in
its appearance but by nature is always illusory. Leaving self
behind is not negative spirituality built on self-rejection. It is
not about repression but liberation. To leave self behind means
shedding unnecessary or harmful baggage: to travel light. It is
to be liberated from obsession, self-fixation and the maze of
desire. Leaving self behind is opening the gaol cell of the ego
and stepping out into the vast space of spirit and the freedom
of the children of God.

IN THE SILENCE of prayer, we unhook from the ego to
reconnect with the pure, sweet space of our true Self. We
re-centre from self-fixation, self-consciousness, self-obsession
into liberty of spirit. A self-fixated person cannot love and so
cannot live fully. A selfish person cannot be happy. There's
a lovely Buddhist text that sums up Mahayana Buddhism:
'All the unhappiness in the world comes from people who are
trying to find happiness for themselves. All the happiness in
the world comes from people who are trying to make other
people happy.' Like all wisdom it is universal.

July

FINDING HAPPINESS BY freeing ourselves from the gravitational force of the ego? How do we do that in meditation? In a simple way, by ceasing to think about ourselves and finding a stronger gravitational force. Simple, not easy to do. It is not easy to give up thinking about ourselves because we are so locked into a worldview with ourselves at the centre. In meditation the perspective shifts. A quiet earthquake happens and we find a new alignment of our attention in God. I don't mean we are thinking about God. We are giving our attention to the living God way beyond our ideas and images about him. To say it again, meditation is not what you think.

ONE DAY I was giving a retreat in the US trying to describe meditation to the audience. Then I noticed somebody sitting in the front row wearing a t-shirt with a loud printed message which summed up what I was trying to say. It read, 'Meditation is not what you think.' I can't remember whether it was a quote from me or someone else. It's not original. I asked the person wearing it to stand, turn around and show their shirt to the crowd.

BEING NON-POSSESSIVE MEANS practising detachment. If you come to me and say, 'I've lost my watch and I really need one, can I have yours?' I ought immediately to reply, 'Sure, here it is.' The way of detachment is fun and challenging when you also have to live in the real world. Interaction with others continuously confronts the root of our possessiveness, our difficult friend, the ego. If we can't teach this friend how to let go, we become possessed by our possessions. But if we unhook from egotism we have already renounced all our possessions.

OVER THE YEARS I have spoken with many married people about their marriage. It is not so different from community life. You may be married to the same person for ages and get through most of life with them. Yet, as time passes you may find you are both on autopilot and have stopped paying attention to each other. Then you might conclude that love has drained out of the marriage. Love may need new expressions to stay alive. Paying attention is giving yourself again, listening, telling the truth, and this can rejuvenate an old love. There is no magic bullet but I know many couples who have started to meditate together discover they can do this.

THE MOST OBVIOUS thing about a teacher is that they need to know or understand something we don't. It should be useful knowledge, not just information you can get from Google or a course. After his enlightenment, the Buddha was challenged during a teaching session by a man who said, 'If you're so enlightened and you know everything, tell me my name and tell me where I've come from.' The Buddha said (more or less): 'It's true. I have seen the light but I only know what it is necessary to know.' A true teacher knows what is necessary for us. A spiritual teacher shares their self-knowledge.

6 July

ANOTHER CHARACTERISTIC OF a teacher is that they want to transmit what they know. It is perhaps their true desire. They are not guarding their knowledge for themselves. If I know something and keep it to myself instead of offering it to you, I am exercising power over you. Knowledge can be seen as this kind of power, as we see in our present 'information age'. A teacher does not equate knowledge with power. The teacher empowers by sharing what they know. At the Last Supper Jesus said to his disciples, 'You call me Lord and Master, and rightly so, for that is what I am. But I call you friends. I call you servants no longer. I call you my friends because I have shared with you everything I have learned from my Father' (John 13.13; 15.15). Everything. Empowering.

7 July

JESUS TEACHES UNIQUE knowledge that he needs to transmit to humanity in friendship. He is limited only by our capacity to receive and learn. He sees our potential to be a friend. Friends are equal. A friend is open with you and desires only good for you. 'I call you friends because I have shared with you everything I have learned from my Father ... so that my joy may be in you and your joy be complete.' He is describing the transmission of himself, of his Spirit.

FOR ANYONE WHO feels that Jesus calls them to follow
him as disciples, his teaching, his Word, enters them. They
are lifted to another level of relationship with him: 'Christ in
you'. This is how we understand Jesus as 'saviour'. The word
means protecter, healer. His early disciples saw Jesus as the
'Divine Physician', not as a judge or moralist. He heals the
universal wounds common to humanity.

JESUS SAVIOUR AND the Cosmic Christ. There is a challenge
in harmonising these two ways of seeing him. In Christian
art, the Cosmic Christ was often shown like an emperor on his
throne looking down fiercely on everyone. It was a politically
influenced image. But the Cosmic Christ is not an imperialist
Christ, even if the institutional aspect of the religion that came
to bear his name sinned through complicity in oppression and
colonialism. The Cosmic Christ has universal presence, not

imperially through external force but *interiorly*, through the transforming power of love. St Paul harmonises the titles when he says that the 'secret is this: Christ in you, the hope of your glory to come' (Col. 1.27).

10 July

THE COSMIC CHRIST is the Inner Christ, present everywhere and in everyone. When I know the Christ in me, I know him in you and I am beginning to see the Cosmic Christ. In the Upanishads, there's an unforgettable description of what is found within the heart, which resonates with what I am failing to say. 'At the centre of the castle of Brahman, the human body, is the heart; and in the deepest place of the heart, there is a flame, the size of a thumb; and in that tiny space, are all the worlds, the whole universe, everything that is.'

11 July

THIS DAILY WORK of stillness and silence is not just for ourselves. It would be foolish if we ignored the wider, ambient consciousness of society and the urgent needs of the world. The more intensely we go into this work, the more we cannot fail to sense that we are part of a great work of the Spirit today raising global contemplative consciousness to a new evolutionary level. Every meditator in all traditions is part of this work. We are beneficiaries and communicators of it. We do it for ourselves and for everyone else. Contemplative practice is a universal work and the most unique personal work we could do. We can meditate with others and we can teach it to others but no one can meditate for us.

12 July

MEDITATION IS A universal and a personal work. It connects us to the cosmos, to the Earth and to other human beings. First, though, it makes us more familiar with ourselves. The Tibetan word for meditation is *ghom*, which means 'to be familiar with your mind'. If we are not familiar with ourselves, how can we be at home anywhere or with anyone? And of course, meditation connects us to God as the ground of being. Some great spider spins the web of reality everything belongs to. Nothing exists without first coming to be in the web of Be-ing.

13 July

THE PSALMS ARE great poetic literature. They describe the wide spectrum of human feeling and our responses to life, from light-hearted joy, wonder and praise to dark despair. Jerusalem is one of their recurrent symbols, transforming the earthly city with its turbulent history into a sign of a heavenly Jerusalem, our true peaceful home. In the Book of Revelation, a moving vision of this archetypal city is described. No temple is necessary there because God is now fully revealed. Religion with its potential for division is absorbed in the sacred reality itself. Cities are human creations and combine diverse groups. *We* are this amazing City of God. We are a community of embodied being. Embodied and embedded in the mystical Body of Christ.

14 July

AT TIMES WE suffer intense turbulence and distraction in mind and feelings. We may even wonder if we are losing our mind. The City of God seems to have fallen into chaos. But even that cannot erase the stillness at the centre of the city of the self. It is from that stillness that the knowledge of God arises to restore peace to the noisy streets and suburbs. 'Knowledge of God' is an ambiguous phrase. It means our knowledge of God as well as God's knowledge of us. They cannot be un-entwined. Our knowledge of God is a small key opening the way to the beautiful city of God's knowledge of us.

15 July

THERE IS NO more important priority for religious people than to reduce to silence our self-generated fantasies about God and ourselves. They go together: you cannot have a fantasy about God without having a false sense of self. If you suffer from false ideas of self, based on self-rejection, self-hatred, self-doubt, it easily becomes self-destructive or self-hating. In this sad state we have lost ourselves as an image of God and so we are going to see God with the same negativity. Our knowledge of God and our knowledge of ourselves are two sides of the same coin of consciousness. We cannot know God without knowing ourselves.

16 July

THE WORK OF the mantra is demanding. It is spiritual work just as going to the gym is a workout in the physical realm. As it develops the muscle of attention, it increases our mental agility and clarity. That is progress we can see quite quickly. In every kind of work we do regularly, we become more conscious of what we are doing, more attentive to the people we are with and more responsible to our environment, interior and external. Although the times of meditation are not the whole of our life, they do become the centre, the catalyst, for heightened attention in everything we do.

17 July

THERE IS A road sign that warns drivers, 'In case of breakdown wait for recovery.' This is good advice for the inner life too. What is recovery? It is reclaiming the wholeness that we have painfully lost (maybe also *necessarily* lost). Rediscovering is the desired result of all losing. We have to want to rediscover it although we may have no idea how. Recovery is healing and by regaining the wholeness we lost we become more whole than we were before. Recovery or healing does not mean going back to a time before we were wounded. It means paying care and attention to the wounds we have suffered and which steer life to its next stage of evolution. Eventually it takes us to the end of the story. We will know it is the true end when we can clearly see our beginning in it.

18 July

HOW DOES MEDITATION aid recovery? In a simple but radical way. It cuts through the overgrowth of memories and prunes the images of desire. When we let go of images, the cycle of desire is interrupted. If we break out of the cycle of desire, even for a short time, we break a pattern that controls us. If we continue to break it regularly, it will eventually dissolve. Then we recover what we have lost – our wholeness, hope, innocence or sense of goodness. We can then restart with a new beginner's mind. This is, of course, death and resurrection.

19 July

IN THE CHRISTIAN tradition the experience of purity and wholeness is called the 'prayer of the heart'. The heart is a symbol of more than interiority or emotion. In all traditions the heart symbolises the embodied spiritual dimension of wholeness, integrity and the process of personal integration. It is in heart-consciousness that the physical, mental and spiritual dimensions of ourselves find unity, harmony and integration. Language expresses this in many familiar expressions: whole-hearted, from the heart, heart-longing, broken-hearted, open-hearted.

20 July

SOMEONE REBUKED ME recently for speaking too much about social issues and not just sticking to spiritual ones. I replied that a contemplative community needs to have a concerned, engaged attention to the world, including its sufferings, challenges, conflicts and divisions, whether they are political, personal or social, whether the issues are social or economic injustice or prejudice against minorities. As contemplatives, we should be actively aware of these issues and, if we really are contemplatives, we will not find we lose our contemplative practice because our attention is engaged in this compassionate way, because of our thirst for justice. Our compassion and hunger for justice will intensify our life in the Spirit. This kind of engaged contemplation is the gift that we contribute to our contemporaries. Contemplatives must be contemporary, ever-present, now. The person who had rebuked me did not look convinced and ended the exchange.

Maybe for him contemplative spirituality suggests an escape from the world. For the Desert Teachers it was not an *escape from* but a *flight to*.

IF YOU ARE truly attentive to someone, you are loving them. Inspiration for this insight is Jesus' teaching: 'Love one another, as I have loved you' (John 13.34). That is, pay attention to one another just as I have given you my attention. The act of voluntary attention is the very heart of consciousness. The need for this intensity of consciousness is felt urgently in all aspects of our global crisis. It is the first order of priority if we are to survive to build a better world. Healthier ways of loving the planet, the fields of social justice, the care of the young, education and the threat to democracy – all these need a contemplative mind capable of dissolving polarisation and reconciling opposites.

THE TRADITION THAT we belong to is a living transmission of the Holy Spirit. It has helped humanity to evolve over eras of time and can help us today to face all manner of dangers and risks. At the heart of this tradition of consciousness is the wisdom of contemplation developed through meditation. The simplicity of a personal daily commitment to practise calls us to enter our 'inner room' and be touched and transformed at all levels. Without practice, it is all mere words, even if they are beautiful words. Without this practice, meaningful words quickly dissolve and silence is forgotten when true conversation becomes screaming.

23 July

I HAVE OFTEN SPOKEN about the 'levels of consciousness' that meditation exposes and takes us through. As soon as we start to meditate, we become more aware of ourselves, more conscious of how we are made and how the mind, the body and the spirit are meant to function integrally, in a peaceful harmony. This harmony arises from self-knowledge, which is a kind of knowledge very rare in a chronically distracted culture like ours. But it is essential and urgent for us all to recover it. Without it, we cannot experience the transcendence necessary for seeing God which is the real-life purpose of the human being.

24 July

SAINT IRENAEUS SAID, 'The glory of God is the human being fully alive.' And, he added, 'The life of the human being *is* the vision of God.' God is glorified whenever the human flourishes. When this happens, it is not as we imagine it will be. Fullness can be felt through all that life continually presents to us. As life unfolds, the vision of God reaches higher degrees of fulfilment. It is like a dance. At first it seems as if you only have the dancers but as the dance gets going, you realise there is only the dance.

25 July

EVERY EVENING DURING the pandemic we heard the Covid statistics and many experts talking about what the figures meant. We need statistical analysis but it is not to be confused with what Blake called the 'holiness of minute particulars'. This holiness is present in the few who give their whole attention to the unique person they are with at that moment. Simone Weil says the greatest act of generosity that we are capable of is to listen wholeheartedly. It mirrors Jesus saying, love one another, pay attention, listen, care for each other, as I have listened and paid attention and cared for you.

26 July

WE SIT STILL with back straight, close our eyes and try to say the mantra; and within micro-seconds we find ourselves scanning our menu of problems, shopping lists and daydreams. Our minds are exposed in their fragmented, untidy, untamed, wayward and uncontrolled state of distraction. This applies even for people who, professionally, may have formed good powers of concentration and an ability to concentrate on technical things – like a doctor or lawyer or teacher trained over many years to focus their knowledge and skills. Generally, everyone who meditates discovers how distracted they are. Meditation reveals human equality as well as our uniqueness.

27 July

DISCOVERING OUR DISTRACTED state of mind, at the first level of consciousness, is a universal experience. One of the first things we say to the MBA students we teach (and who are intensely keen to succeed at meditation as at everything they do) is, 'Give up the idea of success as soon as possible.' Then giving up the idea of failure is much easier. The ego must confront both these ends of the spectrum of self-assessment. I cannot sit and say my mantra, as I would like to, from the beginning to the end at this first level of consciousness. But I can keep trying. Remember Sam Beckett: 'Fail, fail again, fail, fail, fail better.'

28 July

SHARING MEDITATION AS part of our Christian tradition of prayer is a gift to the one who shares and the one who receives. It also allows all other forms of prayer to be better understood. I think it is important in the Church (and in all religions because this is something that affects us all) that we communicate the truth that at the heart of our spiritual life there needs to be an experience of pure attention, pure prayer, of contemplation. Even though, at first, we may feel as if we are failing at it, we have to keep trying and we need to encourage one another in this learning process of non-denominational discipleship.

WE NEED MUSCLES, physical muscles, to lift or to stretch; and we need attention to be able to focus, to love, to listen, to attend to the needs of others, to learn, to understand. Without attention, the healthy muscle of attention, all these essential human aspects of growth – focusing, listening, tending to the needs of others and our own needs, learning what we don't know and understanding the mystery that we are part of – all of this can be lost.

TO CURE OURSELVES before more extreme damage is done, we need to understand how we became such a distracted civilisation. We suffer increasingly from an inability to make the healthy, lasting relationships that demand selfless attention. How can we make such a relationship if we are only thinking about ourselves? In small, simple steps and daily practice we can learn to take the attention off ourselves, which is why meditation manifests in all our relationships through the first fruit of the Spirit: love.

MORE AND MORE clearly, at least as it seems to me, meditation is not an optional extra for children entering the kind of world that we have prepared for them. It is an absolutely necessary life skill. In front of screens from an ever earlier age, a child's powers of attention are often damaged, perhaps irreparably, from the outset of life. Even a baby has remarkable powers of observation and openness to new experience. A child, however, needs training and space to develop these gifts to the full. If the child is too restricted in the isolation of screen-reality and exposed to too much stimulus, spending too much time in front of a screen, then the result is obvious: this damages their capacity for learning, for wider wonder and surprise, for solitude and even for relationship.

August

1 August

GENEROSITY INSPIRES GENEROSITY. Attention is the most generous gift we can give. Saying the mantra is an act of generosity, paying attention to the word without demanding or expecting anything in return because all our attention is in the act itself, the act of saying the mantra. What makes it so pure is that it is purified of egotistical desire and self-consciousness. Little by little, we reach this purity and grow into it. And as we grow, the fruits of the Spirit inevitably appear.

2 August

IN THE SECOND chapter of John Main's *Moment of Christ*, he writes about how to deal with distractions. These are two points he makes. The first is to ignore the distraction, not to negotiate with it or flirt with it, but just drop it. This begins to develop an inner discipline of stillness. The distracted mind is constantly moving, cruising, shopping, ever restless, and we will feel this even physically when the mind is in this state. When you are churned up emotionally it is difficult to sit still and no posture will feel right. You want to jump up and do something. But if we ignore the distractions (by returning to the mantra) as they arise, we develop the quality of *hesychia*, one of the key words in the contemplative tradition, meaning simply 'stillness' or 'silence'. The second point is: do not evaluate yourself.

JOHN MAIN USES a classical image in mystical literature, of cloudy water settling and becoming clear. When it is calmed and clarified you can see to the depths, even to the ocean bed. Gregory of Nyssa, really a mystic for the Christian meditator, uses this image beautifully in his writings when he describes how the journey takes us through the darkness of unknowing. When the mind is turbulent or opaque, its true depths in your own being are hidden. You are washed away by your mind-waves of thought. But as you ignore that, and as the mantra leads you to stillness, a greater clarity emerges and you can see into the depths of your own being. Here you see because you are seen and known and you see that you are seen by love. This is the beginning of real self-knowledge. With it comes self-acceptance and healing.

HEALTH, WE MIGHT say, is more wisely understood as the experience of wholeness that incorporates even what seems like its opposite – sickness, suffering and even death. These are normally said to be opposed to health. And it is true we naturally want to remove them – if possible. If it is not possible they need to be accepted and incorporated into a fuller understanding of wholeness. Acknowledging and accepting them doesn't mean you look for suffering, but acceptance and inclusion when it is there is essential to the healing process. It leads us through the paradox of reality to the greatest wholeness and most flourishing health.

5 August

SURELY, DEATH AND aging are experiences of the nature of reality that bestow a unique and new approach to life's meaning. If we deny the fact of death or aging, or of any kind of suffering, we close ourselves against meaning, which is our experience of connection to the whole and is the lifeblood of the human journey. Growing in acceptance of reality and in existential understanding of meaning are two of our major sources that connect us to reality, to God as the ground of being.

6 August

HOW CAN YOU measure love, joy, peace, patience or kindness? Nevertheless, you can recognise and experience them. They teach you, in your own experience, that you are changing and that these qualities are signs of the life of the Spirit at work in you. Even if you cannot recognise them at first, the people you live with tell you.

7 August

THERE IS A connection between the notions of health and salvation. *Salve* means a healing ointment. It is rubbed in and works as it is absorbed through the skin. There is a connection in the play of words here that illuminates us when we meet them in the personal experience of healing, in our own discovery of what the health we value so much really means and through our own manifesting wholeness. Meditation helps us to see life as a journey of healing to wholeness, and to see holiness as our sharing in the life of the One who is holy, the One who is one, the One who is whole.

LIFE OFTEN DAMAGES us; it can unexpectedly throw us off balance. Great losses, or great mistakes, or the aging process, disappointment of hopes, or a broken relationship – any of these things is going to hurt us one way or another. Maybe they will strongly destabilise us or shake our self-confidence or make us feel we may never make a new relationship after such a great loss. Life itself needs continuous putting together again, reintegration and many new beginnings. This healing of the wounded psyche is part of what we call integral health.

THERE IS ALWAYS growth potential in our basic capacity for awareness. You can be aware of somebody in need but it could be an objectifying, cold-hearted awareness. Such awareness has the capacity of upgrading to attention. This is personal, relational attention to the unique needs of the other person. Other-centred attention naturally moves further up the scale and overflows into compassion. It tends towards self-less action as the sense of unity becomes undeniable.

OUR EXPERIENCE OF deep wholeness that we have at times in meditation, and in fact of integral health, takes us far beyond the narrow, medicalised definition of health by the World Health Organization – which says something like the 'complete absence of pain, illness or suffering' and invokes a kind of utopian state of metabolic efficiency. 'Integral health' incorporates suffering and even death. It reminds us we can and should die healed. This opens a more realistic way to understand why we should want to stay healthy, eat well, do exercise, sleep enough, have a balanced life. Meditation will help you form this kind of attitude to health without fearing you are becoming fanatical or flaky. There is no health in just having a slim, fit body if your mind is sick or you are unhappy in your marriage. Health covers all these other dimensions: the physical, the psychological and the spiritual.

MY TUTOR AT Oxford surprised his students at a dinner party one night when he asked us what was the most pleasurable thing we could think of doing. We replied in various ways meant to make us sound clever or unusual. Then it was his turn and sipping on his port he said, 'Falling asleep, when you are so exhausted there is nothing else for you to do but put your head on the pillow and go out.' I was not meditating at this time but now I might say, 'Meditating when it's the time and your mind is calm and there's nothing else you would prefer because it feels the totally right thing to do.' At these moments when we have no choice but to do something we find delicious we are perhaps at our happiest because we are at one with our deepest desire. We do not have to scan choices. Our choice has found us.

12 *August*

WITH PRACTICE, YOU will find that you can start to meditate full of anxiety, stress, fear and general distraction; but at the end of the meditation you can get up in a remarkably clear and calm state. The problems you started the meditation with are still there but the effect they have on you has changed dramatically. You may think, 'What was all the fuss about? After all, I can handle this, and if I can't handle it then there's nothing I can do anyway. So why make myself miserable about it?' With practice you will find how meditation has this wonderful gift to calm and clarify the mind and emotional system and restore our nourishing link with wisdom. Like any art, and meditation is an art, it has to be learned and practised with love.

13 *August*

WE SIT, WE come to physical stillness and alertness, we close our eyes and begin to repeat the word. All we are asked to do during the meditation is to keep repeating the word with minimum effort, with gentleness and fidelity and to return to it as soon as we are distracted. It is truly as simple as it sounds. It is not a mechanical but a creative and faithful repetition. You say it simply without evaluating yourself. Life is full of minor repeated routines and chores, doing the laundry, paying bills, doing the dishes. If you perform these mechanically and unwillingly or grudgingly, they will frustrate and anger. Meditation may teach you to no longer see them as boring and time-wasting. You will become a contemplative washer of dishes and clothes or even a mindful commuter.

14 *August*

LONELINESS IS ONE of the scourges of modern culture. It is one of the heavy prices we pay for affluence in the First World. It is a competitive world, where the human is often reduced to mechanical systems and endless evaluation and targets to achieve. Loneliness comes with always being competitive. (The word 'competition' comes from a Latin root that means 'seeking together'. How did we move to making it mean 'fighting each other'?) Loneliness can be a problem even for people with loving support around them but is most likely when we are living in a state of physical or emotional isolation. The cure and antidote for loneliness is solitude. Meditation teaches us what solitude really means.

15 August

THE CHALLENGING PARADOX of a spiritual path is that we take the attention off ourselves in order to find ourselves. Most of the time, however, we are focused on ourselves, our problems especially, whether external, like deadlines we have to meet which cause stress, or interior, like the relationships that fail or turn toxic. A high level of stress and anxiety is understandable, given how we are brought up and manipulated. As a result, most of the time we are thinking about ourselves or evaluating our happiness or lack of it. Until we learn otherwise, it can make us desperate because we assume there is nothing we can do about this unhappy condition. We can learn that there is something we can do.

AT MANY POINTS along the 20 to 30 minutes of a meditation, your attention will falter and you will become distracted by external or internal concerns. If you can get ten
minutes into the meditation before you become distracted,
you are doing well. Be faithful and you will find that, without
trying to do better, you will. Being faithful means that, when
you are conscious that you have stopped saying the mantra
and are distracted, drop the distracting problem-solving or the
fantasising and return to the word. The mantra is a narrow
little path through the jungle of your mind. When you wander
off the path into the jungle and become conscious of it, get
straight back on the path. However long you have spent in the
jungle of distraction, you are never more than one step from
the path. At first, distraction feels like failure. But actually, as
you return to the path the failure becomes a teacher.

EVENTUALLY, WE WILL come to the point where we do
not make a big deal about 'this was a good meditation,
this was a bad one' because you know you are simply being
faithful, not trying to succeed. When you get to that point,
where you are detached from whether it was good or bad, it is
then, in the detachment, that your meditation is really taking
you deeper. So, it is not about evaluating 'success, failure', it
is doing it faithfully without judging, without attachment to
the results. That is progress. Do you see what I mean? The
measure of progress is your detachment from the idea of progress.

I LIKE TO REFLECT with people about the importance of
reconnecting today with our contemplative tradition. The
link between the questions of holiness, human holiness and the

holiness of God, has always been a key issue of this contemplative tradition This is why I also like to speak with people about meditation. It is the best way I have found to answer the question. The answer can only very inadequately be put into words. But the experience is a clear and simple answer to what holiness means. Each time we meditate we step into the zone of this contemplative tradition and experience its wisdom for ourselves. It is a way into a daily life that rests on contemplation. People sometimes ask, what is the difference between meditation and contemplation? The simplest answer I can offer is: meditation is the work we do to receive the gift of contemplation.

19 August

WHAT DOES JESUS say about prayer? The first thing he says, in the Sermon on the Mount (Matt. 6.5–8) is: 'When you pray, go into your inner room.' What does that mean? The heart. 'Close the door and pray there where your Heavenly Father is, and you will be enriched and rewarded.' The ground of being. Not the idea of God, but the real presence you find and that touches you in the inner room. 'God is the centre of my soul,' John of the Cross said. So interiority, finding your centre, is the first element of Jesus' teaching on prayer.

20 August

THE SECOND ELEMENT of the teaching of Jesus on prayer is becoming the silence that includes everything. It is based on faith that God knows what we need even before we can ask. Faith is foundational. Living in faith involves a shift of consciousness that will inevitably influence your beliefs. It also begins a shift in our notion of the nature of Christ. Silence does not mean discarding intercessory or petitionary prayer or prayer for healing. It means that we stop thinking that our asking is about either informing God of something or asking him to change his mind. Because of this, we could say there are no forms of prayer, only different ways, more or less direct, into the mystery of prayer in which we, the one praying, are the first to be changed.

21 *August*

THE THIRD THING Jesus tells us about prayer is 'do not worry'. Do not be anxious about what you are to eat, what you are to wear. Instead, he says, look at the beauty of nature, the lilies of the field, the birds in the air. Contemplate the beauty of your own nature. Know yourself. To comfort people in distress we sometimes say, 'Don't worry.' It is well-intentioned but rather too late. Yet we all like to be reassured and consoled. But that is not what Jesus is doing. 'Do not worry' is a call to us to stop being controlled by our anxieties and problems. To drop them. We may have worries and anxieties but we can leave them on one side during the time of prayer. If we say, 'I can't,' still try and the trying will become a cry for assistance that will not be ignored.

THE FINAL THING that Jesus says about prayer in this section of the Sermon on the Mount is: be in the present moment. Don't worry about tomorrow. Again, this is neither a platitude nor cheap consolation. It is a wisdom-teaching on how we should be at the time of prayer: be in the present moment here and now. God *is* and I *am*. All time is eternally present in the God whose being we enter here and now when we pray according to the teaching of Jesus. So then, if you combine these elements of Jesus' teaching on prayer, what do we have? We have interiority, silence, equanimity, single-pointedness and the present moment. Put those into the blender called daily practice and you have a delicious drink called contemplation.

'CONTEMPLATION IS THE simple enjoyment of the truth.' You could also say that contemplation is a panoptic view of reality. Panoptic – seeing all sides. But seeing all, not with scientific coldness or objectivity, but with love, wonder, tenderness and delight. The more points of view you see, the more inclusive and compassionate you become. That is contemplation. That is what Jesus is teaching. The essential work and commitment of self we make in this teaching is to pay attention.

MEDITATION HAS TO be freely chosen; no one can force you to meditate. They might force you to go to church, but they can't force you to meditate. And it is an ascesis because we develop our capacity for attention in a gentle but specific and faithful way. It is so much more than just relaxation or stress-management. The goal is the peace that passes understanding, the great *shalom, salaam, shanti*. It is what we begin to taste from the beginning of the journey and that we become more one with as we travel deeper.

25 August

IT IS NOT attractive to us but it *is* necessary that, at the right time and with the right support, we can face into our own unconscious, all that we do not yet know consciously about ourselves. We can do so, overcoming fear and resistance, and find that these negative energies are transformed into states of pure energy and wonder. We need help to stay balanced to travel to our centre. Ultimate balance is integration with the centre. The centre of the human being? The heart. We need to be already some way into the heart, grounded there, to have that stability and equilibrium to be open to the wonder of what we do not yet know and who we will become when we know it.

26 August

FEAR ASSUMES MANY irrational shapes and stratagems and so it is hard to deal with at a rational level. If we overcome our fear of the unconscious we can then plunge into the unconscious as a place of encounter with God. To overcome fear is to learn to love and be loved. Perfect love casts out fear. Perfect love means total attention. When we are sure that we are receiving pure attention, fear dissipates and eventually evaporates. As it happens, we become imperceptibly empowered to give total attention. Instead of the darkness of fear, we see everything by the light of love.

27 *August*

EVENTUALLY, IT BECOMES all about union. But until union is complete, we continue to think of it as relationship. Me and the other(s). True relationships teach us that they never cease to take us deeper through many losses and apparent finalities. Relationship, as we know from all kinds of intimacy, involves degrees of turbulence and conflict. There is much suffering on the road to union. Meditation, which is all about union from the beginning, teaches us important and useful lessons for dealing with pain and loss. It takes us through storms by releasing the gentle power that is bringing us all along towards the end relationship in a union so perfect it is divine.

28 *August*

THE FIRST GOAL of all spiritual practice is equilibrium between the conscious and the unconscious. It is not the balance usually attempted by repressing the unconscious and protecting us from what we fear. Religion can easily become an agent of repression, reinforcing our familiar way of seeing the world but secretly protecting us from God's way. This kind of religion is really anti-God. It doesn't want God involved at all because it actually wants to keep God out. That is why religious people can become so ungodly when the whole of their religious observance is dedicated to suppressing the Spirit of God that is moving in our unconscious, our deeper levels of consciousness. We are frightened, without good reason as it turns out, of what will emerge if we cross from one level to the next. Some of the demons that we have suppressed, our fears or traumas, will emerge but only to release us from themselves, not to destroy our sanity.

29 *August*

IN THE FIRST pages of his book *Word into Silence*, John Main, who was my teacher, said he hoped the reader would be helped to find a teacher. I think many readers do not notice this and hope the book by itself will be the teacher of the information or skills they need. Early in our journey, Fr John helped me, as only a teacher can, to see how essential it is to transcend our individual conditioning. We are more than the product of our cultural or psychological histories. By transcending, however, he did not mean destroying. Nor does it mean adopting a new off-the-shelf persona as many first-time pilgrims to 'the East' do on their return to the West. Only a teacher who has done it can really explain it. It means an ultimate liberation as expressed in *sannyasa* or monastic renunciation of status and possessions. Transcendence is radical detachment which leaves us not, as we fear it will, an empty husk but a playful child of God. It is a great and rare gift to have found a teacher.

30 August

UNIFIED CONSCIOUSNESS IS about incarnation, embodiment in the here and now. It is becoming fully, sustainably present. How often have you said something only to find a few moments later that your listeners were not listening? How many times have we tuned out when we should have been paying attention? We practise in daily meditation to face our divided minds and to reunite them in the miracle of attention in the present moment.

31 August

IF WE DON'T reconnect with the wisdom of unified consciousness and learn to see the human family as interdependent and coordinated, our extreme global suffering can only get worse. It will affect rich and poor alike but, most grievously, it will attack the most vulnerable. Covid gave us an idea of what simultaneous, disruptive globalised suffering could be like, like a world war or global financial crisis. For most of us, comfortable enough for now, and lacking first-hand experience of war, displacement or famine, it is hard to imagine. We risk falling into denial or complacency. This is the unique moment in history we all share and we cannot fail. Dire as it seems, the danger can unite humanity as never before. In that unity we could find the peace we have been looking for from the dawn of human consciousness. Crisis brings opportunity. Dark nights end in the dawn.

September

1 September

THE HUMAN MIND likes to take everything apart and analyse it: to contrast light with dark, sweet with bitter, good with bad. We listen, nod and then say, 'Yes, but'. To understand what is good we need to have experienced what is really bad. Even when we have tasted the peace of oneness, the wisdom of non-duality, we must still live in a dualistic world. Dealing with the denial of paradox plunges us into a world of endless contradiction with its violent divisions. This occupies a large part of human life and awakens us to the need for a contemplative practice if we are to survive.

2 September

AFTER THE SEPARATION of light from darkness, when the Word was spoken in the eternal beginning and all that ever came into existence appeared, the Book of Genesis describes the great separation. It has never stopped since. After primal unity came a breathless, intoxicating diversity in nature. 'The earth yields fresh growth' and 'the waters teem with countless creatures and birds fly above the earth across the vault of heaven'. When God saw all this, did he say, 'Oh no, what a complicated mess I've made,' and rewind back to primal unity? No, God gazed lovingly and 'saw that it was very good'. The beauty of the cosmos is that what is separated seeks its origin in unity. It is the terrible beauty of God.

3 September

LITTLE CHILDREN LEARN arithmetic and one of their first lessons is division. I was hopeless at maths but I remember the rush of happiness accompanying a change of perception when I discovered how division and multiplication work – or just that they existed. The ability to do division is of practical importance for a child as it ensures that everyone at a birthday party will get an equal slice of the cake. There will be loud cries of protest if it is not divided equally, just as the ancient prophets were outraged when the wealth of the nation was distributed unjustly. Division is a sign of wholeness, of equality, and underpins the exchange and barter of life that shapes every society and family.

4 September

IN THE NOCTURNAL darkness of the Easter Vigil, illumined only by the single flame of the recently lit Easter candle, we listen to the ancient chant of life, the Exultet. It contains the paradoxical words, 'O *Felix Culpa*' – O Happy Fault (or Fall or Guilt) – 'of Adam'. Happy, because it necessitated the coming of God in human form. From darkness light, from shame dignity, from guilt restitution. God brings good from evil. It is both a theological and a magical insight that a greater good comes out of the worst evil. Julian of Norwich, too, penetrated the darkness to discover the same truth that 'sin is behovely'. This means it is necessary and inevitable. Whenever we feel depressed by our failings or the dark forces raging in the world, we should recall the wisdom of this theology. Or if you don't like theology, listen to one of those sudden, disturbing disharmonies in Bach which he inserts but then uses to reclaim a higher beauty and joy.

5 September

AS HIS LIFE drew to its close, Jesus saw in the mounting forces of division, deception and violence that the 'prince of this world is coming'. But he added, 'He has no power over me.' In the inflamed consciousness of the dualistic world, he entered his Passion centred in the unified and unifying consciousness that he had discovered in his young life. His oneness with the Father revealed his unity with all. Dying into this union he found himself fulfilled – 'glorified' as the Scriptures say – and he returned as promised in the new dimension of reality we call the Resurrection.

6 September

WHEN OUR MIND and heart are unified, we become clear enough to see the essential goodness of our being undimmed by our imperfections. 'The eye is the lamp of the body. If therefore your eye is single your whole body will be full of light' (Matt. 6.22). When the eye of the body and the eye of the mind are unified, the third eye opens. With the eye of the heart, we see why our sins are 'behovely', and our faults happy. We see – even if fleetingly – the whole picture and how everything belongs in it.

7 September

CONTEMPLATIVE CONSCIOUSNESS IS the result of a unified mind and heart. It restores health to society because with a single eye we can see beyond dualities and polarities and resolve their conflicts peacefully. If we can see across the chasms of division those with whom we can no longer converse, we see and feel differently about them. The most secure common ground is not found in politics but in this spiritual dimension. Everyone can know the healing of the single eye. Anyone who experiences it knows it to be a power of wise tenderness that can melt divisions.

8 September

WE ARE HOLY. But it is never 'my' holiness. It is always 'ours'. This is the great teaching of the mystical Body of Christ – *our* body. The source holiness is the One who is holy, who says, 'I am who I am' (Ex. 3.14). I think it is helpful to remember that we do not have to *achieve* or *earn* holiness or grace. It is already here. How close is the Kingdom of God actually? Jesus said it is not far from you: only a step away. It is not distant or above our pay grade. We simply have to trust and to give it a chance. The chance we are giving it is our daily practice to let the mind be silent, still and simple.

9 September

THE WORK OF meditation is the work of the mantra. It is a demanding discipline but we are fortunate to have found it. Like daily exercise, it is real work. But it increases our springiness of the mind so that we can develop the muscle of attention, the capacity for attention. And we notice that very quickly, in everything we do: we become more aware, more attentive to the people we are with, to the environment we are with, and more aware and attentive to what's going on within us as well. Meditation isn't the whole of life, of course, but it does become very much the centre of our life if we see our life as the journey into attention, into love.

10 September

ATTENTION IS REALLY another word for love. When we pay attention, we have taken the attention off ourselves; the centre of consciousness shifts from its usual self-centred, self-reflective, self-fixated position to actually being turned outwards to the other, whatever the other may be. Other-centred. We move from being self-centred to other-centred; that is the real movement of life as our journey to God. That is divinisation. No wonder regular practice teaches us that meditation is at the centre of our whole process of living.

11 September

JOHN MAIN CALLS the unfolding experience of daily meditation a journey, a pilgrimage. It is a pilgrimage, because it is a journey to a sacred place. That sacred place is our personal, unique point of union with the Mind of Christ, which opens us to the mystery of the Father. Grace more than willpower allows us to make this journey, to persevere and humbly start again while accepting ourselves as true but imperfect pilgrims. Grace is the Holy Spirit.

12 September

AND THEN YOU discover that this very childlike way of becoming silent and still, coming out of our head and entering the heart, is simple but not easy. Why is it not easy? For several reasons. One of them is the fact that we are attached to our stream of thoughts and imagination, and ideas and images. We are heavily attached to these because that is what we think being conscious means and that is all there is. Loosening our attachment, our grip, on the content of our minds is therefore quite disturbing. It is saying there must be something else but I cannot see it yet. So, for some people it's quite frightening and they give up after five minutes. For others, it is like being handed a key to freedom and using it.

13 September

MEDITATION WILL HELP to break patterns of obsessive, compulsive thinking. They may be feelings of insecurity, thoughts of anxiety, spasms of fear. But you lay aside them all. They are all 'thoughts'. There are other kinds of thoughts. You may have thoughts like 'Oh wouldn't it be wonderful if ...' or 'Won't I have a great time when I do, get or achieve this in the future.' You lay aside these thoughts of the future as completely as you do with thoughts of the past. The mind is like a factory in 24-hour production. It's going to be continually producing material and it expects you to package, market and consume all that material continuously. Meditation is a way of discipleship to the truth in which we need to retrain the mind and teach it a different way.

14 September

JOHN MAIN SAID this to me right at the beginning of my journey: 'Nothing happens during your meditation, and if it does, ignore it.' He meant that if I started looking for something to happen during the meditation, I would be looking for the wrong thing and when the real thing happened, I wouldn't recognise it. Of course meditation is a process of change and so things happen in and outside the times of practice. But don't look for *experiences* in the meditation. Act as if nothing will happen and you'll always have a full tank of gas and a clear road in front of you.

15 September

WHAT DO I mean by contemplation? And why does meditation lead us into the state of contemplation? Well, Thomas Aquinas defined contemplation very simply as 'the simple enjoyment of the truth'. The simple enjoyment of the truth. You couldn't get more simple than that. It is simply finding joy in what is. The truth doesn't mean a dogmatic or scientific explanation or definition of reality. The truth is what is, in all its dimensions. Even quantum physics, as it explores the mysterious and invisible aspects of the world in its infinite relationality, is discovering more and more dimensions of reality. So does the meditator.

16 September

EGO, YOU COULD say, is a sort of an image or rough model of the true self. It is a kind of consciousness, but only a fragment of consciousness. It's like a light bulb, but with a dim wattage compared with the true self which is blindingly bright. 'God is light.' So the ego, we could say, serves a useful function of separation and communication but, if it is allowed to believe that it is the self, the true self, the whole, then we have problems. Because then it begins to act as if it were even God, as if it is the centre and the ultimate expression of reality – what I feel, what I want, what I imagine, that must be the truth. As a famous Twitter (X) user used to say: Bad!

17 September

THE CAPACITY TO pay attention is at the heart of human development. If as children we are trained to be aware of the feelings of others – for example, that if there are other people in the room we should not scream or bang the door, that we should be polite as we enter or leave a room – these simple basic elements of courtesy, civilised behaviour, are really qualities of attention. If we learn them they develop higher qualities of attention in us. We will intuitively listen to a person we do not like, and even respect points of view we consider wrong, and attend to the needs of others. But if we lack that basic discipline of attention that must be learned young we will be in grave danger of becoming totally ego-centric personalities.

18 September

THE ULTIMATE TEST that the ego is tamed and in its right place is that we lay down our life for others. That means we give our attention to others and can recognise the suffering that others carry even when that suffering is the result of their own wounded ego. This is what is meant by loving one's enemies. It is easy to love friends who love you. It is easy to love people who are in a state where they just require help that won't cost you anything, when they are passive, hopeless and helpless. That is relatively easy. But to love those who are rejecting you, cancelling or defaming you, that is the test of true love. We will fail many times but we should never stop trying or believing this is the Way.

19 September

FEAR IS SOMETHING quite specific. I am frightened of failing my exam, I'm frightened of being knocked over by a bus, I'm frightened the operation I'm going to have will not work. These are specific fears. Anxiety is different. It is a vaguer sense of dread, of feeling that something, whatever it may be, could happen any time. We are walking through life as if it were a minefield. Anxiety is a chronic condition, non-specific, but it is another form of fear to which we can attach our phobias and resentments. The ego's acutely separate sense of self is activated by fear and it can become trapped in the condition of chronic anxiety. That, of course, produces stress and all the by-products of stress. Meditation de-stresses us because it casts out fear with the energy of love.

JOHN MAIN SAID that meditation is the prayer of faith because we have to 'leave ourselves behind before the Other appears, and with no pre-packaged guarantee that he will appear'. So here is why meditation seems risky. It is the risk we take whenever we love and declare our love. It is the core risk of being alive: leaving self behind 'before the Other appears', without guarantees. Meditation is a pure act of faith. It is a repeated act of faith if we meditate seriously – that is to say, regularly. With practice, faith soon becomes an act of love.

WHAT BEGINS IN faith turns into love through faithful repetition. Keep repeating something faithfully, and if it is something positive, if it is other-centred, it will lead to love. If you keep repeating something that leads to isolation and fear, then clearly this is not an act of faith, it's an act of addiction or compulsion. There are different kinds of repetition. There is faithful repetition and there is mechanical, involuntary or forced repetition. Meditation is repetitive, but it is *faithfully* repetitive.

SAINT IRENAEUS SAID, 'The beginning is faith, the end is love. And the union of the two is God.' Great little formula. It is as good and true as e=mc². The truth is always simple. The beginning is faith, the end is love. Faith plus love equals God, and love, as we know, casts out fear. 'God is love. Whoever dwells in love is dwelling in God and God in them … There is no room for fear in love. Perfect love banishes fear. Fear brings with it the pains of judgement. And anyone who is afraid, has not attained to love in its perfection' (1 John 4.18).

LOVE DISPELS FEAR and we must then learn to live without fear. Over time, the effect of meditation is that as fear reduces we become less frightened. Eventually, or at times, we can feel and act fearlessly. When we do, it strengthens the confidence of being who we are. If fear reappears, even in its former chronic form, it is more easily recognised and controlled because we know that if it can be mastered once it can be again. This is the process by which meditation reshapes the ego. It trains the ego so that it becomes less of a tyrant and more of a vehicle to love and serve others.

BOTH THE WAY and the goal of meditation are found in the resetting of the ego. The end is here, so is the way to the end. Liberation from fear and its illusions, healing of the wounds of life stored in the ego's memory, are part of the journey. The ego only becomes dysfunctional because of this memory of painful separations and loss which produced its own self-defensiveness and self-inflicted wounds. But as the ego is healed of these stored memories that have wounded us for so long, it finds a healthier, more natural way of functioning. It becomes a bridge rather than a security compound and because it is no longer frightened of others it enables us to be of service to them.

25 September

I WAS ONCE DRIVING in the southern US when a pickup truck drew alongside me and the driver and his companion looked angrily at me. They shouted 'Loser!!' at me in a very unspiritual way. I had no idea what I had done to deserve it until I told my friend whose car I was driving. He said, 'This is Texas.' He was an Obama supporter and declared this on a bumper sticker. Lose and find. Lose to find. Choose to lose. We can lose by letting go of attachment, whether of an ego-image or a self-centred ambition. Of course, we also lose by forgetting and as we live longer, we are more likely to experience this in dementia. Failure is an enforced loss as we cannot, strictly speaking, choose to fail. The fruits of loss, however, are plentiful provided we learn its lesson. They are found in self-understanding and self-acceptance and in enhanced relationships. Instead of seeing others as an ominous threat to our identity, we now see ourselves – as losers! – in them and them in ourselves. Experience becomes something more than a way of reflecting ourselves. It becomes translucent, a two-way seeing. This permits the one we are seeing to see themselves in us. Let's hope they like what they see! Even if they don't, divine seeing is active in the human Mind of Christ. God sees himself in us when he sees Christ in us. When people shout 'loser!' as an insult there may be more to it than they can see if they would like to discuss it.

26 September

IN OUR UNHAPPY world, there is a multi-billion-dollar industry of happiness and well-being. However, most of its products are rather depressing because they assume happiness is a goal to achieve, whereas it is our true nature. The secret of happiness is free but has a high cost in terms of self-realisation. It is released in the right use of freedom, respect for others and their points of view and in commitment to justice. The best example of true happiness is the life of Jesus but I have seen it reflected in many people and occasionally in myself. These qualities make us *fully* alive and happy. They fulfil the conditions of happiness described in the Beatitudes. 'The glory of God is the human being fully alive,' said St Irenaeus.

27 September

WE MAY THINK, 'I don't have time to meditate but I am very aware of everything and practise attention even when I am multi-tasking. Actually, I think I need multi-tasking to feel awake.' This is a delusion of hyper-active minds, too much flitting from task to task, dependence on distraction. Brief, rapid TikTok bursts of stimulation might appear as if attention is being exercised. In fact, it is being dissolved. The muscle of attention is atrophying. It needs silence, stillness and silence combined, the therapeutic exercise of pure prayer. Contemplation is our greatest need today and we need to give it time.

28 September

JOHN MAIN SAID that if we spend three or four hours a day watching TV it will be hard to meditate seriously on a daily basis. He warned of this before the age of the internet – on which people in our time (aged from 16 to 64 years) spend an average of seven hours a day. This adds up to 17 years of their life. Today Fr John would no doubt warn against mindless browsing or being grafted to your phone. If we want to change anything in our life, it becomes more than a question of will-power. If we really want to change, we need to allow a greater depth of consciousness to arise in us. With that, we will see more clearly what we must do to change. Seeing is believing and then we will truly *want* to change. With that new depth of self-knowledge we will be able to truly want what we want.

29 September

OVER TIME AND without realising it, we can become self-centred, ungenerous, acquisitive, protective, posses-sive, even nasty people. This is not just the result of possessive love but of fear, which is the opposite of love. Fear imprisons us, narrows our range of experience and crushes the joy of life. We become like rich people who are increasingly terrified of everyone they see as a threat to reduce or confiscate their wealth. A truly generous person can overcome fear because they know that the real riches of life are in the gift of life itself – not what we have but who we are, that we exist. These riches are immeasurable, inexhaustible. They are increased by generous loving. In this sense every person is super-wealthy. Whatever our tax bracket, we can give our attention to everyone we meet. The quality of generosity of our attention increases with practice. This wealth is poverty of spirit and the dividend is the Kingdom of heaven.

30 September

IN NATURE, FRUITS come at the end of a growth process, each stage of which has to be respected. When we sit to meditate for the first time and discover how it is simple but not easy, and how distracted our minds are so that we feel like jumping up and running away, we just have to accept it. For now, it is what it is. Whoever introduced us to the path should have prepared us for this. But then we move to the next phase of growth.

October

THE GROWTH OF a contemplative community is achieved in simple ordinary ways, by living in the present rather than by ten-year plans. Living daily life in the spiritual dimension first affirms that such a thing exists, to begin with as an aspiration. With commitment in faith to this hope, the community becomes a channel, a window, a portal to the spiritual realm, as its members become more awake. In this dimension of faith, we undergo transcendence, able to be other-centred and to take the risk of loving. Community can only really be understood by those involved in living it.

2 October

AS WE LOOK into the depths of our soul and see the wonder of the cosmos that is there, the mystery of God in the ground of our being, we are surprised by joy. But also challenged by it. Do we really want this kind of joy? Yet life without the mystery is flat and meaningless. Mystery is a real encounter with the living God. Reverence awakens us for the scale of wonder and for the laws of nature and the subtle truths of the spiritual dimension beyond our understanding or control. Wonder opens our heart to the simple fact of something and we feel the suspension of our faculty of comparison. Reverence brings us to our knees as we glimpse the coherence of the laws of the universe – the Tao – as we know that we are intertwined with them.

3 October

LOVE IS THE highest knowledge. Erotic attraction can cloud the mind and make happy fools of us. But love without the desire to possess or to find gratification except in the happiness of the beloved shows us completely who they – and we – are. It verifies the fidelity of faith and of the indwelling of the Holy Spirit revealing we are participants in the great dance of being. The force that flows into and from and between Father and Son also pours incomprehensible light onto the true identity of Jesus the Christ. Completing the cycle in which all life flows, the human Jesus has released, activated, opened the floodgates and breathed this spirit of truth into and between us. This is the heart of Christian insight, that the Holy Spirit lives in each human being, acting in any form but limited to none. And meditation, as John Main says, 'verifies these truths of our faith' in our own experience.

4 October

WE CALL MEDITATION 'pure prayer' because we are not doing it to please God, to get something out of him by his fulfilling our desires. Meditation delivers us from this childish imagination and takes us to a higher imagination towards a story we cannot fully comprehend. It changes our understanding of 'Ask and you will receive'. It is the pure un-opportunistic prayer that asks for nothing and gives everything. It is the gift of contemplation, of paying attention to God not for the benefits we get but because it is good, authentic and delightful in itself. Only humans in the universe as we know it can meditate. Even practised imperfectly – 'very humanly' – it intensifies and expands our humanity because in our poverty we know God's loving attention to us.

5 October

WHAT MAKES US fall in love with someone and continue to fall? Is it seeing their innocent desire to be fulfilled and accepted and feeling that maybe we can fulfil it for them? Of course we seek our own fullness too, but not as our primary motivation. Seeing the same longing for fullness in another makes us recognise them in ourselves and ourselves in them. It becomes the great equality in otherness. When we truly see this pure aspiration in another how could we exploit them to fulfil ourselves? We are entranced. And so, we fall in love and keep falling by recognising in them their potential and attempt to find fullness of being. It is the first fruit of the Spirit and the mystery of love.

6 October

MEDITATION IS THE most natural thing in the world. With other natural things like food and water, good work and beauty, we need its nutritional value to become fully human. If life fails to open this spiritual dimension in us we feel incomplete, chronically unsatisfied. Meditation, which as I have said is simply a way of love, can address what life has failed to do yet. Love is not only a feeling but a direction we face and move into. It is where we place our attention. We do not know where to place it but we begin by taking our attention off ourselves. This summons the descent of the Spirit. St Paul gives love first place in the scale of virtues: it is the light, the moisture, the nutrition that allows all the seeds in us to start the process of bearing fruit.

7 October

OUR PRACTICE IS connecting two levels of consciousness. At the superficial level we discover how distracted we are while at the deeper level we experience something we do not know how to name at first. In time we see it is the stroke of love. A lover we never expected to find in ourselves. The bridge between the two levels is attention – the choice, the work, the mystery of attention. It enhances our feeling of what being human means. And in an age of such dehumanising forces of consumption, technology and bureaucracy, meditation becomes a particularly necessary and effective way to protect and affirm the human. It shows us we are not helpless or hopeless: we *can* turn our attention to the people we are with and to what we are doing. Nothing in the animal world or the digital worlds can compare with this human capacity to make love by giving attention.

8 October

COMMUNITY THAT ARISES from contemplative practice, the work of attention done together, shows us the global nature of the Church as the one Body of Christ. The scandals and self-fixation of most religious institutions today fail to do this. Beautiful buildings, ceremonies, dressing up in magical clothes, separating clergy and laity, all this does a disservice to the wonder and mystery that religion can make visible. Without contemplation, religion becomes stale and unappealing. St Peter was talking to a group once when the Holy Spirit 'suddenly descended upon' his listeners. In churches today there often seems a design to keep the Holy Spirit from interfering in what is going on. No institutional form can ever be expected to mediate the Spirit without a corresponding receptive depth of authentic interiority.

9 October

'SO PUT ON the garments that suit God's chosen people – compassion, kindness, humility, gentleness, patience' (Col. 3.12). This dressing up in natural virtues reminds us of all the fruits of the Spirit we encounter in our own experience of meditation. The first fruit is love, which grows simultaneously with the deepening of the spirit of attention. The more we strengthen the muscle of attention, the more loving we are. *Be forbearing with one another*, this text goes on to say. Be patient with people who disappoint and irritate you and fall short of your expectations for them. Control the expression of your disappointment and anger (I have learned slowly); prevent separation occurring between people because of their different points of view. True tolerance in our polarising world is a fruit of patience and forbearance.

10 October

WHO DOES NOT recognise the ego in themselves when it surges? If we don't, then we will learn quite soon after we start to meditate. That is one of the first buds of self-knowledge we find. I find helpful the idea of a breakthrough. For example, we break through the wall of the ego as we pass through all levels of consciousness on this journey of self-knowledge into the Mind of Christ. What are the first questions anyone asks when they start to meditate? How long does this take? How long before I reap the benefits, how can I feel confident I'm not wasting my time? As we break through these questions we see that what we fear we have missed is already present.

MANY PEOPLE BECOME disappointed and discouraged because they think they are not making progress. Or they give up too soon, often just before a breakthrough happens, because they cannot understand why they feel dry and unfruitful. Or, if the introduction to meditation did not prepare them for the stages of the journey, the meditator gives up when the going gets tough. In the WCCM, we feel it is of first importance that the introduction is clear and complete. From the first step we try to share a realistic understanding of the potential of the practice. The basis for this introduction is not lots of ideas, however, but the support and friendship everyone needs for a long, variable and beautiful journey.

FOR ST BENEDICT there are three pillars supporting the human condition as a journey to God. There is prayer in different forms but always pointing to the prayer of the heart. There is work which can also have many forms, although for Benedict it was primarily manual work. The third pillar is *lectio*, reading to nurture the mental and imaginative inner world with good content, not just entertainment. Sacred scriptures, music, art and good conversation all nourish the soul. These three human elements reflect the integral wholeness of body, mind and spirit. Each is distinct but belongs to the others.

I OFTEN SPEAK OF the different levels of consciousness we pass through, to harmonise, heal and integrate them on the daily journey of meditation. There is the monkey mind, the hard disk of life-memory, and the brick wall of the ego. When we hit the wall, it feels as if we are permanently blocked. 'I will never get any further. How can I break through? I meditate every day and no breakthrough is happening.' When our spirit sags, who does not need a little help from their friends? We need to be regularly encouraged and this is what any spiritual tradition provides through community and good counsel. Not just encouragement to 'come to church' but to stay on the contemplative path. Churches should be offering this as it speaks of prayer to children and adults alike. They should be places where an unusual wisdom resides that recognises how prayer works; it knocks the bricks out of the wall. Faith moves mountains and brings about personal and social transformation. Prayer is not wish-fulfilment but glorifying God through human transformation.

14 October

JOHN MAIN'S MODEL of the self is a biblical model of the body, the mind and the spirit. It is shaped and grounded practically through his teaching on meditation. He puts contemplative practice at the centre of his working model of human life that is on its way to divinisation, returning home to its source in God.

15 October

REMEMBER ST PAUL on the gospel as a 'way of salvation that begins in faith and ends in faith'? A *way*, not a technique or a club or an ideology, but a path, a way of living, of healing, flourishing and of coming to spiritual vision. Fullness is immeasurable, so the way must be open-ended. So, what do we mean by faith? Something different from belief. Even the Devil believes in God. We are not saved by belief. Jesus often said to those he healed, 'Your faith has healed you. Go in peace.'

16 October

AS WE SIT at the wall of the ego, saying and listening to the source of the mantra, as attentively as we can, returning to it faithfully when we slip away in a distraction, something happens. We cannot see it happening objectively but we know it. This is a simple, childlike practice that we come to love because it opens us to love. Little by little, it changes the way we see the wall from a menacing blockage to a stepping-stone. Meditation changes, but does not destroy, the ego. We need a healthy ego for many things, including its being the stepping-stone we leave behind.

17 October

THE MEANING OR deep connection that we need for fullness of life is not found in concepts, rules or answers. Life is greater than a problem. It needs truth and truth is the whole, all-inclusive. Words may evoke it but cannot capture it. Meaning is the knowledge that we are connected to a greater whole. People often describe meditation as like coming home. We come safely home, feel welcomed and embraced by the deeply familiar and fully recognise the place for the first time.

18 October

GROWTH AND EXPANSION are breaking-through moments. They require faith, commitment and perseverance, at many levels and in all the areas of life. Meditation is a catalyst for this. It is a contemplative practice built into ordinary life, morning and evening. Every contemplative practice that is a catalyst to growth in us awakens this process of expansion by allowing us to commit and to be faithful in everything great and small. So we find we can put our whole heart into everything we do.

19 October

SOME WORDS OF John Main from his book *The Way of Unknowing*: 'To awaken is to open our eyes. And we open them, as St Benedict said, to the divinising light. And what we see, transforms what we are.' This describes the process of breakthrough. I am not referring to breakthrough just as one big event. Sometimes we do have big moments of revelation, dramatic changes of consciousness, and we see everything is transformed. But the breakthrough process is life itself, like a river flowing towards the boundless sea. It is one stage of development after another, with many corrections of our course. We are continuously breaking through into the next stage. Fr John describes it here as awakening and don't we wake up gradually? First thing in the morning, we see blurrily and rub our eyes to become more awake and conscious of our surroundings. Meditation is like that, opening your eyes to see more clearly.

20 October

SAINT JOHN SAID, 'We do not know what we will be like in the future, but we know we shall be like him, because we will see him as he really is' (1 John 3.2). Learning to see God is the essential human experience of divinisation. It is ultimate meaning. To see God *is* to become God as only God can see God. If that sounds New Age, it is. A new era of consciousness dawned with the Christ event. Becoming aware of this, amazed, the early Christians and their teachers began to understand its implications. Subsequently, the Church became less amazed, more banal, focusing on ideas rather than experience. As it grew in size it became more distant from the experience. 'God became human so that human beings can become God' is, however, both the oldest and freshest Christian insight.

21 October

THE 'BREAKTHROUGH' IS a continuous unfolding and expansion of consciousness in love. The other phrase, 'spiritual life', can be deceptive. It simply means life as a whole because life *is* the spiritual journey. We do not have to fit in spiritual practices, juggling them with other priorities, but we do need to cultivate the conditions which allow the good soil of our being to bear fruit. Like planting and caring for organic growth, meditation is a natural process. It is as natural to our spirit, meaning our essential nature, our true self, as breathing is to the body.

22 October

A GARDENER, LIKE A true healer, *collaborates* with nature, learning and respecting the laws of nature. As meditators we do the same. We follow basic laws and come to understand and revere the particular laws within the integral spiritual dimension. The meditator, like the gardener or healer, obeys these basic laws of reality. A basic level of obedience is giving the time necessary for contemplative practice.

23 October

SPIRITUALITY IS NOT about gaining spiritual experiences or gaining anything at all, more about letting go or refreshing our perception of what is there. It is not about reading about other spiritual experiences and wondering if we will get them. That is a tempting but false, because second-hand, spirituality. Of course, we need the example and teaching of others further along the path but they call us to our own mature uniqueness. It is like enjoying films about the natural world without ever going physically into nature, whether a wilderness or a park or small garden to *see* and breathe it in. Every day. Spirituality is made authentic too by life-balance. It means cultivating our own small part of the great field of human nature. In that field, if you remember the parable of Jesus (Matt. 13.44), the treasure of the Kingdom is buried, waiting for us to discover it.

24 October

A CONTEMPLATIVE CHRISTIANITY REDISCOVERS and renews sacred Scripture as nourishment for the life-journey. Contemplative practice awakens within each person, and also within communities and society at large, a fresh understanding of what spiritual experience means. Sacred Scripture then comes alive as we recognise *it* because it comes directly from this same experience. The primary Scriptures

– not sermons that are disconnected the same source as our own experience. Religion without contemplation is blind. Contemplatively-fed religion will not confuse external religiosity with the personal participation, through the grace of contemplation, in the divine source.

25 October

THIS IS HOW Dante ends his great poem *Paradiso*, the culmination of the *Divine Comedy*:

> As a wheel turns smoothly without jarring, my will
> and my desire were turned by love, love that moves
> the sun and the other stars.

They are his last words before Dante is absorbed into the vision of God. It is the final transcendence of the suffering, darkness and negativity of the unconscious he had explored in Hell and Purgatory and it is his release into pure wonder, praise and delight: awakening to the mystery of the first power in the cosmos that transfigures all other forces into itself, the power of love. Source of life, nourisher of life, goal of life. Little by little, every meditator comes to see their practice as a journey into this still point of the power of love. It is the turning point of the wheel, the centre of equilibrium releasing the power of union. 'Be still and know that I am God' (Ps. 46.10).

26 October

SAINT PAUL SAYS, *this Spirit of God is the spirit we have received*. It is an unsettling affirmation that, when we are within our own spirit, we encounter the Spirit of God. As we come to know ourselves, we discover the Spirit of God is the self-knowledge of God purposefully, lovingly, tenderly, relentlessly, calling us into itself. Thus our spirit, that is our self-knowledge, becomes one with God's self-knowledge.

Perhaps one way to describe it is like the merging of what is fully conscious with the less conscious. Under the laws of the spiritual realm, our spirit progressively moves into the orbit of the Spirit of God and life as a spiritual journey takes off on a new trajectory. This is the fulfilment of our deepest desire.

27 October

TODAY WE ARE all fed, saturated, with news true or fake and strident views and opinions. In contemplation we are fed from the source, that is ever-new. Opinions, even cherished beliefs, yield to the pure air of the spirit. As it opens itself to us, we are drawn back to the source of consciousness itself. Mystical wisdom traditions call this source the heart, the apex or 'virginal point' of the soul. Medieval mystics liked to say that this is the one place the Devil cannot get into or look into. We might express this insight by saying that ego is always frustrated when it tries to muscle into the heart-centre. It is prevented from seeing what is going on there because it cannot understand it. Like a cat put out of the house, the ego shrugs and goes off looking for something else to do.

28 October

CONTEMPLATION IS THE primary and universal source of wisdom. But there are other sources that satisfy our thirst for truth. Indigenous cultures have deep wisdom as a source from which we can – and need to – drink. Nature itself, when we immerse ourselves in a natural environment, is another source. The human body, in sickness and in health, always tells the truth because the body never lies. It is always in the present moment. When we are well attuned to the body, mind and spirit are in harmony. When we are one with the grounding sacrament of our body, we experience it as another primary source of wisdom, a physical sacrament of our true nature.

WHAT DO I mean by 'contemplation'? And why does meditation lead us into it? Thomas Aquinas defined contemplation as 'the simple enjoyment of the truth'. Could you get simpler than 'the simple enjoyment of the truth'? Finding joy simply in what is. The truth cannot be captured in dogma or by the scientific method or theological definition of reality. The truth is *what is*, in all its dimensions. And as quantum physics explores the invisible world in its interrelational nature, it is discovering more and more dimensions of reality. Nevertheless, truth gets simpler the more fully we experience our unity with it.

CONTEMPLATION IS SIMPLE. It embraces and embodies all that is and may yet be. All dimensions of reality. All points of view. All sources of wisdom. All cultures. All faiths. Surely, this must be what the teaching 'God is One' means. In some ancient wisdom traditions, it is said that creation arises directly from God's meditation. God is contemplative and we can only know God when we enter the state of contemplation and ourselves become infinitely simple.

'UNLESS YOU BECOME like little children, you will not enter the kingdom' (Matt. 18.3). We become childlike when we meditate. Depending on where we are starting from and our historical baggage, it will be more or less an uphill struggle at first – at times – but the sure sense of being on a journey will grow stronger and more energising. We do not need to worry about how long it will take because we only need to begin and keep beginning. Keeping to the starting point with a beginner's fresh mind is all we need. This is an understanding of meditation and an incentive to begin that the Christian contemplative tradition needs to declare with strong conviction in our aching world.

November

S ET YOUR MIND on God's Kingdom before everything else and everything else will come to you as well. A way to set your mind on the Kingdom is to say the mantra. After each meditation, the problems and anxieties that you began with will feel different and more manageable. With more layers of consciousness in order and experiencing detachment, greater space opens for the fruits of contemplation to appear. The things you once pined and begged for will come to be in ways that will take you by surprise. This is accumulative, of course, which is why contemplative practice, as the very practical St Benedict understood, needs to be regular. Let nothing be preferred to the work of God, he said.

T HE SIMPLE ENJOYMENT of the truth. I find this such an astonishing insight it is hard not to keep coming back to it. Consider contemplation as a panoptic view of reality. Panoptic means seeing all sides at the same time but not with a coldly objective vision. The way of seeing is far beyond that because it is a detached view from the inside of what we are seeing, seeing with love, tenderness, joy and wonder. The more dimensions of reality we see, the more whole, the more inclusive and the more loving we become.

3 November

THE PHILOSOPHER WILLIAM James, founder of American psychology, said, 'Reality is where you place your attention.' Quality and direction of attention matter. In our distracted culture, whose members spend an average of seven hours daily on screen, very young brains are deeply affected. This is a fragmenting of our core capacity for the kind of attention that makes us human. Attention is our ability to listen, to be empathically aware of others' feelings, to engage compassionately, to see the wonder of the world 'in good and bad alike'. Attention is the essential work of meditation. However distracted we may be when we begin, it strengthens the muscle of attention. Attention is also the essence of prayer. So, meditation is about training our mind and heart in tandem, the two inbuilt sources of wisdom in our consciousness.

4 November

LISTEN TO THE shrill, hateful condemnations of social media, conversations collapsing because of constant interruptions, the us-and-them universe we have imagined into being. We should be looking for regenerative sources of wisdom, not just complaining about 'the crisis' and who to blame. We should be seeking all these many sources of wisdom and linking them to each other. Each spring of wisdom draws from an underlying water-table, a unified body of wisdom and benevolence which we can call the Spirit. Wisdom is one. It may manifest and touch us through many sources: indigenous cultures, poetry, science, music, sacred ritual, mystical transmission within a spiritual community or through the beauty of the world or a child's smile.

5 November

IT IS ALWAYS worthwhile to examine one's motives for doing something, including why we meditate. For example, is it just to relax or to achieve privileged knowledge that sets you apart from the crowd? It will be difficult to persevere with either of these as motivations for daily practice; nevertheless, the practice will correct your motivation and any egocentric reasons for doing it will gradually dissolve. Through practice, you will come to different ways of knowing. Rather than just giving you more information about yourself, it will reveal the knowing that *is* your self. In one of his poems ('Cure at Troy'), Seamus Heaney uses the phrase 'utter self-revealing'. It means an opening from within which astonishes us with a new depth and clarity of knowledge, not self-reflective but a blend of knowing and being known that rises and breaks through all our ignorance and nonsense.

6 November

A NECESSARY CONDITION FOR allowing the break-through process to happen is patience, the ability to wait peacefully in hope. Because of the impatient, grabbing culture we are conditioned by, we have forgotten the disciplined art of waiting that reduces anxiety and prepares us for what will come. We demand that what we want is delivered *now* and we would speed up even the processes of nature if we could. To relearn the art of waiting and to be one with nature is neces-sary to save our humanity and our home planet. It can easily be taught to children at a formative age if we, their teachers, are sane enough to know how. Creative solutions begin with urgency and patience. Teaching meditation to the young is one such creative response to our time.

REALITY IS ALWAYS *breaking through*. Even when we block or deny it, preferring false consolation or self-destructive indulgence, reality builds up and eventually overflows all resistance. This can be very painful. Developing the active capacity to wait in active stillness prepares us more gently to recognise and welcome reality. It is no less than our collaborating with the power of God to manifest in us in new ways that respect our limited capacity. We are all impatient because on this side of the wall of the ego, our ability to taste reality (wisdom *is* tasting it) is still weak. Immersing ourselves in unnecessary activity and thought supports the fantasy that we will get what we want when we want it.

8 November

METANOIA, CONVERSION OF heart, moves us from false simplicity to real simplicity. The real thing comes from undivided consciousness in the state of non-duality. However, experiencing this does not make us less able to function in the dualistic world. It is not about being angelic or impractical. Seeing ourselves in others and others in ourselves actually helps us to live and work better in the world. When we are grounded in simplicity, we cannot act with cruelty or inhumanity or prefer to build walls rather than bridges. We are less likely to act like this because it is unnatural to do something false while seeing the truth. We need contemplative consciousness in daily life in order to create the more just, humane and more peaceful society we aspire to.

9 November

WHAT ARE WE turning towards, if we turn our heart to another person? God is the ever-present other and we meet God in every other person in the world. If we turn towards the person we are with, we are pointing ourselves towards the unified state of undivided consciousness. 'May they be one as you, Father, and I are one. You in me and I in them, may they be perfectly one' (John 17.21). At the heart of Christ-centred seeing is the discovery, the self-realisation, the breakthrough into the field of undivided consciousness, of oneness. The sign it is happening is that we, our feelings and thoughts and our lives, become simpler.

10 November

WE ARE EACH of us designed for the contemplative life which includes finding our unique work in life and fulfilling the responsibilities attached to it. As the *Bhagavad Gita* says, happy is the one who finds their work and the work of silence and who knows that silence is work. Modern values have devalued and monetised work into a financial exchange of time and labour for status and reward. So much in our society has become primarily about money and success, earned at the expense of others rather than for their benefit. Good work makes us healthy and human. Good work brings out the best in us and brings benefit to others.

11 November

JOHN MAIN'S TEACHING invokes the Golden Rule, a universal expression of wisdom found in all spiritual traditions. 'Treat others as you would like them to treat you' (Luke 6.31). This involves a big change in our behaviour but it happens naturally at a certain moment in the development of contemplative consciousness, as I suddenly see myself in others and others in myself.

12 November

TODAY I AM on Bere Island, a place I love and belong to. There can be many weathers here every day so I don't come for the sun. Like me, you may find that your daily mind can be as changeable, even as turbulent, as the wintry weather here today. Atlantic storms have been drenching us constantly since I arrived for a time of solitude. I love it. Then, this morning when I opened the curtains, I looked out on a calm, sun-soaked landscape of sea, fields and mountains, a cloudless sky and a playful palette of joyful colours. 'What a wonderful world,' Louis Armstrong sang, and Shakespeare added, 'O brave new world that has such people in it.' Life is an ever-surprising series of epiphanies and each one helps us to wonder at the total gift of life.

13 November

OUR MIND FINDS peace only when we can fully accept what we experience, uncomplainingly and with detachment, whether the experience is painful or pleasant. Only this full acceptance shows us how to be real by rejecting denial and fantasy. Through experience, life teaches us that reality is one. Rain or shine, pain or pleasure, failure or success, losing or finding, death or life. No one part of the paradox of reality stands alone. Everything touches everything in the seamless experience of the one reality.

CONSIDERABLE TIME AND effort are required to achieve that *victorious surrender* when metanoia transforms us, in the sunshine of reality, and burns away ignorance and delusion. It is not easy but it is easier than not being faithful to the process once begun. On life's inescapable, relentless journey every step then opens us to deeper degrees of peace.

WHY DOES IT sometimes seem so hard to commit to the path of metanoia and stay on it? We may have moments, in meditation or at other times, of clear sky bathed in the sunlight of love. They are so powerful they feel they will never stop. Even when they pass, we have learned something we cannot forget. Weather changes, the mental sky is clouded again by thoughts and delusions. The pain of loss and doubt undermines what was once certain. We are creatures of time. But through the loss and lesson of letting go comes a quiet conviction, called hope, that we were not deceived.

16 November

THE UNPREDICTABILITY OF the weather of life is why we should fix the roof while the sun is shining. When storms come, even if the roof leaks again, the damage will be less. Meditation builds resilience. It is a part of our life that we don't have to constantly analyse, but when we miss it we feel the loss. We meditate 'in prosperity and adversity' as the Desert Teachers described how we say the mantra. Whatever the inner weather, we turn up for work grateful that it is in our life. The wisdom of not evaluating short-term, day by day, becomes obvious as the larger perspective of the whole experience becomes clear.

17 November

EVERY MEDITATION IS part of the continuous lifelong experience. For those on our path, the mantra also reveals the *non-interfering* but clear *intervention* of Christ in our life. I mean that he is present but does not take up space or reduce our freedom. Like a personal trainer working to get the best out of us for our own good, he guides us into ever deeper metanoia. Openings then appear in the cloudbanks of delusion. By training the mind we see through these gaps and learn to see inwardly. Gradually, by clearing the obstacles of ignorance formed by fear or desire in early life or through cultural pressure, the eye of the heart opens. We no longer look for God as *some thing* to be found and held. We see God *as* the light by which we see. When the heart is open, what then is *not* God? Metanoia gives clarity and hope even during times of confusion and reinforces the courage needed to keep trying and always to risk more.

18 November

RATHER THAN MERELY introducing new ideas or opinions, metanoia removes false identities and illusions. The simple obviousness of self-recognition best describes progress on this path. It is present in Jesus saying 'Mary' to Mary Magdalene: in the instant of being recognised, Mary recognises him and replies, '*Rabbouni.*' It is the drop losing itself in the ocean as the ocean simultaneously opens to admit it.

19 November

MEDITATION IS A universal gift but also uniquely tailored for each practitioner. Like every gift, it has to be accepted by the person to whom it is offered. Similarly, when we listen to someone with full attention, what you hope for will happen. Your gift to them elicits a response from them. Attention leads into reciprocity. When that happens at the crucial depth, God is born and the Word appears embodied. It is the glory of God manifesting in the fullness of human life.

20 November

WHAT ARE THE signs of enlightenment? One important sign is what the Desert Teachers called *apatheia*, a term meaning 'being without disordered passion'. It does not mean apathy, because it is a highly energised state of human flourishing. It is part of the cycle of growth that we continuously pass through. Life is this cycle of spiritual growth but we can become blocked. When the energy is flowing well, however, we move from the winter of *acedia*, which is discouragement, sterility and depression, to *apatheia* when we come alive again and everything blooms like springtime. The height of summer when everything is fully alive is *agapē*.

IF WE INSIST on only pleasant experiences on the journey of meditation, we will be disappointed. Yet, painful dark nights of the spirit, or periods of acedia, contain seeds of new life. Passing through them, they can be painful, dry, empty, with a sense of loss or abandonment. But these dark times contain seeds of regeneration allowing us to be reborn at higher levels. The reason is that 'everything works together for good for those who love God' (Rom. 8.28).

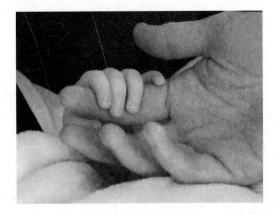

ZEN TEACHING CONCEIVES of both sudden and gradual enlightenment. Maybe they are not exclusive. Gradual enlightenment need not be understood as being slow, but rather as infinite. Every sudden enlightenment has required a long preparation. Experience may feel gradual today but sudden tomorrow, or gradual this morning and sudden this afternoon. Gradual and sudden really refer to different ways of perception, contrasting views of how we are interacting with the evolving journey itself.

23 November

JOHN MAIN SAYS that meditation is the most practical step anyone can take to rediscover oneself, as more than a statistic, a program or a cog in a wheel, but by knowing oneself as infinite depth of mystery. The contemplative journey of life unfolds through the inner journey of meditation by leading us to self-knowledge of a new order, a unique way of seeing ourselves as a mystery. A mystery is not confusing or contradictory. It is revelatory of a simplicity that can never be worded or conceptualised.

24 November

JOHN MAIN SAID something 40 years ago that is even more relevant to us today: 'We can hardly dare to imagine what a society would be like where everybody was on the road to the realisation that being is mystery and that each of us possesses an infinite capacity, an infinite potential for expansion of spirit into the mystery of God.' Can you imagine a whole society where everyone, or even a critical mass, is on this journey into fuller consciousness? I do not mean that everybody is meditating in the way that I hope these daily readings for the past 329 days might support your daily practice. There are different paths up the same mountain. We are all at different stages. What matters is that we are each and collectively conscious of the journey.

25 November

ONE ORDINARY DAY, Thomas Merton drove from his monastery to Louisville for some errand or other. As he stood on the corner of Walnut and Fourth, he was transported by the awareness that he loved all the people around him and was filled abundantly with the joy of being human. 'It was like waking from a dream of separateness, of spurious self-isolation in a special world.' He longed to be able to communicate what he felt and how he saw them 'walking around, shining like the sun'. What a different world it would be (he thought) if everyone was aware of this. But for him, as for us, such an epiphany moment passes in time. These glimpses of what is real are powerful, unforgettable revelations but they cannot be frozen in time. They are not the end of the journey. Like everything in time, they pass and integrate into the next stage of the journey we are always on.

26 November

WE ARE ALWAYS learning, always in the learning mode, always open to experience. We are not judging or comparing our meditation. Instead, we allow it to be fully integrated into daily life as it becomes a natural part of it. This approach to the discipline opens up the path with ever greater subtlety and wonder, giving a whole new meaning to the word 'ordinary'.

27 November

MERTON'S EXPERIENCE OF unity (I mentioned it two days ago) brightly and briefly illuminated his life's land-scape. Another example of this kind of thing is described in a poem by W. B. Yeats:

My fiftieth year had come and gone
I sat, a solitary man,
In a crowded London shop,
An open book and empty cup
On the marble table-top.
While on the shop and street I gazed
My body of a sudden blazed;
And twenty minutes more or less
It seemed, so great my happiness,
That I was blessed and could bless.

The best advice is 'Expect nothing and demand nothing. But be fully prepared.'

28 November

MEDITATION – LIKE ALL other expressions of love – is non-acquisitive. There is nothing to acquire except poverty, non-possessiveness. The 'goal of meditation' is not to get anything but to lose, to expand the 'let go' mind rather than the 'can do' mentality. It is in poverty of spirit and letting go that we find everything that we truly desire by realising it is already present.

29 November

MEDITATION EVER MORE convincingly shows us that it is a way of life rather than just a technique of prayer or relaxation. And so, if we are concerned by our level of distraction, we should examine our way of life: how we spend our free time, how we work, what habits feed our distractedness. What you want to be like at the time of prayer, the Desert Fathers taught, you should be like before the time of prayer. Meditation will raise wise questions that nothing else can ask us so powerfully.

OUR EGO AND eros-centred cultural idea of love needs to be broadened by the wisdom tradition. This will prepare us for a spiritual understanding that sees love as transcending egoism and integrating eros. It shows love to be creative and redemptive with a trans-personal intimacy. Trans-personal does not mean impersonal, as you cannot have an impersonal love. Love flows from the deepest centre of the person, between persons, uniting persons. It is trans-personal in that it transcends individuality and reveals a uniqueness that silences the ego.

December

MEDITATION IS A learning process, an ever-deepening discipleship (Latin *discere* = to learn). Without fear, self-deception or repression, we learn to face our shadow side, all the self-contradictory dynamics working in us. We mature in this process and function as a more whole and healthier person because we accept responsibility for ourselves and stop blaming and projecting.

2 December

AS WE LEARN how to be poor, we learn in our own experience what the mantra has to teach us. This includes embracing our mortality and becoming free from our strongest repression, the fear of death. Meditation is simultaneously a death and a rising to a fuller life. We accept death and dying as part of life, essential to our growth, and we see non-attachment, non-possessiveness, non-acquisitiveness as our most precious goals.

3 December

SOLITUDE IS LEARNING to accept our uniqueness. That we are utterly unique in the universe can at first be a terrifying insight. Whoever I am, regardless of what others think of me, has never happened before and is unrepeatable. We are who we are. This can only be contemplated if we can see beyond our egocentric vision. To see like this is to undergo an intensive expansion of consciousness, which can be frightening because it means to let go of all that we are clinging to. The fear fades as the experience intensifies and unfolds the true meaning of solitude.

4 December

SAINT GREGORY OF Nyssa was the first Christian thinker to develop the idea of 'infinite degrees of perfection'. Some would say he was the first thinker to understand its importance. To seek God is to find God. Jesus says whoever seeks will find (Matt. 7.7). But Gregory adds that, if it is truly God we are seeking, we never stop finding. There's always more, an infinite series of mountain peaks on an uncountable number of horizons. We never stop seeking. We are on a journey that has a beginning but no end.

5 December

FAITH MEANS RELATIONSHIP and trust within a personal commitment that, once made, goes ever deeper as time passes. John Main said that, along the path of meditation, more, not less, faith will be needed; it will grow to keep us going. The daily practice expands our capacity for faith, revealing it to be our capacity for love. The beginning is faith, the end is love, and the union of the two is God, said St Irenaeus.

6 December

IT IS OF the first importance that we teach a contemplative practice to children and young people while they are setting out on their life-journey. Call it a pilgrim's staff or a life skill. However we label it, it is a gift for life and it is life-transforming. We could also call it an art. Today, if a child left school without knowing how to use a computer, you would say they were not well prepared for life in the modern world. In the same way, if we do not give this art of pure prayer to children, we are condemning them and maybe their children to a future they may not be able to face.

7 December

CONTEMPLATION IS THE *simple enjoyment of the truth.* Simple means beyond analysis or comparison, without planning or explanation or the need to control. If enjoyment becomes subject to any control except self-discipline it stops being joyful. The joy of an artist is visible in the love they feel for what they make. God enjoys what he creates and so loves the world to the point of sharing in its suffering and dark sides. God is the supremely selfless artist. As we pass beyond the control of egoism, we break into our creativity and recognise its source as God.

SIMONE WEIL UNDERSTOOD that, while we must wait for God, without snatching, so too, beyond time, God waits patiently for us to become ready to receive the gift. We see this described often in the Old Testament stories, with disarming naiveté: God waiting until humanity understands who it is and grows up. It will have to stop acting out its ego with the rebelliousness of an infant with its newly formed ego. It seems as if God waits until suffering – both what we bring on ourselves and what is inevitable – finally teaches us. Of course God does not wait – only time-bound creatures wait or get impatient and the divine impatience in these mythical stories is merely our self-projection. Nevertheless, it feels right for Simone Weil to say that, 'God waits until at last we consent to love Him.'

JESUS' THREE CLOSEST disciples, Peter, James and John, accompanied him at important moments like the healing of Jairus' daughter, the Transfiguration and in the Garden of Gethsemane. We may see intimacy as a privilege but it is no less a responsibility and each of us is called to bear it. We have a unique role to play in the Body of Christ and this is framed in the unique intimacy we have with him. No one is second best. The special three were not perfect but saw their intimacy with him as a condition of their discipleship. Disciples begin by accepting themselves just as they are. Intimacy and then union develop by knowing that the loving gaze of Jesus is the call to discipleship.

NON-VIOLENCE IS AN important element of discipleship. It grows naturally as we realise we are loved unconditionally and that we do not need to resort to violence to express our sadness and anger at those we think reject or harm us. It is in the core teaching to turn the other cheek and to love our enemies and bless those who curse us. This is not the way of the world, or how political institutions or nationalist tribes behave. They take revenge, retaliate, get their own back. Some communities achieve the core teaching for a while. But, usually, it is the individual disciple who learns experientially what non-violence means and what it means to change because we learn from the teacher within.

11 December

ANOTHER COMPONENT OF discipleship is to care with spontaneous compassion for those who are helpless or discarded, the weak, the scapegoated, the pawns of power and the voiceless victims of injustice. Our capacity for active compassion is strengthened as we mindfully catch ourselves before we get drawn into destructive gossip or blaming. We recognise the suffering felt by those who have hurt us. In learning these responses, the disciples feel the silent influence of their teacher. Deep, pure prayer releases an unexpected energy of love to care for the uncared-for as if they were ourselves (as indeed they are).

12 December

THE EARLY MONKS who settled in the deserts of Egypt from the third century acquired celebrity, but they were not superheroes. They were mostly simple Christians, people with little or no religious or social status, drawn into living by the values of the gospel: compassion, mercy, faith, generosity, non-judging. They renounced the right to reject those who rejected them. From this monastic movement of simple discipleship comes the teaching on meditation we practise every day.

13 December

AS WE TAKE the attention off ourselves at the times of meditation we become more selfless, more generous, more loving – even just nicer people. We learn to live the essential gospel values by understanding them from within. The meditator begins with the primary value of poverty: the first Beatitude about poverty of spirit. Meditation is about becoming poor in spirit. It is more than about de-stressing or being mindful. These are by-products but not the purpose of meditation. The *purpose* is to become a wholehearted disciple – imperfect but wholehearted.

14 December

THE WORD *MARANATHA* is an ideal mantra. It is an early Aramaic Christian prayer but because of its sound and rhythm can be used as a universal meditation word. If you choose it, say it as four syllables – ma-ra-na-tha – of equal length. Sound the word, rather than visualise it. Listen to it as you repeat it gently and faithfully. Don't use any force; don't try and block out thoughts. Let the thoughts flow but keep your focus of attention on your word. At times it will feel the most simple and natural thing possible. Occasionally it will feel like a lighthouse in a storm. Use just enough effort to be faithful to it. 'Experience is your teacher' and we learn through practice. This art of pure prayer is simple.

15 December

PRAYER IS AN art. The art of arts, as the early teachers said. It is not a transaction, like putting a coin in a machine and selecting what you want. Nor is it an obligation. One comes to love and need it but it is the mirror opposite of addiction. It is an art of love because in practising it we discover that we are loved and by whom. At first it seems as if the mind is scattered and unstable, so it may not feel what we imagine prayer should be. That is a sure sign you are on the path going somewhere. It is a new land we are entering. The Christian mystical tradition – if you study it alongside your practice you will come to recognise and appreciate it – will help you see your personal journey as part of something greater.

16 December

IN 2018 POPE Francis wrote an inspiringly down-to-earth open letter about holiness, *Gaudete Exsultate* (Rejoice and Exult). He said he did not intend it as an abstract treatise or just a theological opinion. He wanted it to help awaken in the reader a desire for holiness. Global marketplaces are full of falseness, such as the false happiness of consumerism which leads to unhappiness and boredom. (There *is* a fertile boredom we discover in poverty before real happiness dawns.) Francis' letter on holiness advances a more authentic set of values. He claims that God wants us all to be saints – complete with happiness and the wonder of life. He says saints are ordinary yet unique people and that we all need to include times of silence, stillness and solitude in our busy daily life.

17 December

GOD, AS AELRED of Rievaulx said in the twelfth century, is not only love. God is friendship: with oneself, others and the environment. Those who are not in friendship know nothing of God. A lack of knowledge of God is especially visible in the cold certainty of religious fundamentalists, convinced they are defending God against his enemies. The more people we identify as enemies, the fewer friends we have, the less we know God. Spirituality in our time is driven by longing for connection and trust, for a true religious sensibility that nurtures community rather than division. The inclusive acceptance of difference releases the real presence. If you really are at home with your self in God you are at home, in peace, everywhere. Then every enemy becomes a potential friend.

18 December

THE DESERT TEACHERS said, 'Pray for the gift of prayer.' This undiluted, non-egotistical prayer is pure. It arises through practice and through life lived in certain authentic values. It is not the product of study or behavioural conformity – being like others. It arises from being turned towards others, and so towards God. This begins with the mantra that unhooks us from self-fixation, which is the principal reason for not feeling fully alive.

19 December

WHEN I GO into the wilderness of Nature, it is like finding a true friend waiting for me. It touches me with the certainty of true friendship that I have countless second chances. Wilderness is a channel of grace leading us back home. Its synchronised life-systems overcome all obstacles to their fulfilment. This determination of nature to be fulfilled might make it seem impersonal until we see we – the human presence – belong. When we feel resonance with the poverty of wilderness, a real (that is to say, reciprocal) presence is released. I am no longer an outsider, an observer. I am at home.

20 December

THE DEFINING HUMAN quest is for our own true nature. Who am I? The heroic task of life is followed through self-transcendence, reduction and renunciation rather than through acquisition and force. It is not merely by the big new achievements but also by loss and letting go – perhaps even more through these – that we are guided to the home destination from where, in time out of mind, we set out in our ever-present origin. It brings us to a startling recognition of the obvious: that it is sufficient to be who we are. But the miracle of being turns destinations reached into new points of departure. As we find we are at home with ourselves (less self-conscious, more attentive to others, more capable of wonder), we become in harmony with all: with every person, every creature and with the boundless world itself.

21 December

SOLITARIES ARE DRAWN to the wilderness but feel fear as well as delight as they enter it. They may look for reassuring signs of civilisation declaring, 'This is the Wilderness. Photography permitted. Do not make fires.' Every wilderness pilgrim is a spiritual pioneer and had to overcome this fear of the unknown when they entered the uncharted wilderness: Elijah and Jesus into the desert, early Christian monks into Scetis and Nitrea, Benedict and Mohammed into their caves, Indian rishis into the forest. The fear of wilderness where there are no traffic lights or shopping malls is the same fear we need to overcome before entering the silence and stillness of the heart.

22 December

THE EVOLUTION OF consciousness from the Origin is driven by our capacity for attention. As attention grows so do our social organisation and culture become more complex. When, however, attention shrinks, becoming self-fixated, human society diminishes and begins to disintegrate. Our present chronic distractedness and triviality, our inability to pay attention or even to remember what we have just heard, are symptoms of a global human malaise and decline. It is partly the result of our failure to control our technology and our lower appetites but it strikes at the core of our spiritual intelligence, which is necessary to respect the values of civilised living.

23 December

IN OUR COMMUNITY we approach meditation Christo-centrically. A Buddhist, Muslim, Jew or Hindu will approach it from their faith orientation. A materialist has their own. Yet, meditation is such an intrinsically authentic practice that when practised from any approach it will be open and respectful to every approach. Meditation opens the common, shared ground without dissolving what is unique and particular.

24 December

O F COURSE, CHRISTIANS can (and should) meditate with the followers of other faiths, including secular faith. They can even introduce meditation to them. By no means does this weaken Christian faith. In fact it broadens and deepens an understanding of the Resurrection and the Universal Christ, showing us that in deep, pure silence we are centred in this person and encounter them. So, we can call what we practise and teach 'Christian meditation' or 'Meditation in the Christian tradition', or, when it is better, just 'meditation'. This flexibility so intensifies the experiential theology of our faith that the multiplicity of ways into the mystery of Christ does not contradict the unity of the one way.

25 December

T HE QUALITY OF being decides the quality of doing. Life teaches us this every day when we fall under the influence of our present mood – sad? angry? peaceful? joyful? This colours how we work, speak to people, chair a meeting, handle the bad manners of a fellow road user, serve at table. Miss meditation and you, and the people around you, will feel the lack of something. A schoolchild once said to me, 'I like it when the teacher meditates with us because she's more patient afterwards.'

26 December

A T THE TURNING point of each year we feel inclined to shed the unnecessary baggage we are burdened with. We look backwards and forwards. Janus (after whom January is named) was the Roman god of beginnings and trans- itions, doors, gates and time. He was two-faced, looking in both directions. There can be moments when we see like this beyond the usual single perspective of time. For me this time of the year recalls both the loss I suffered at the death of John Main and the wonder of what followed, the birth of the World Community for Christian Meditation. It was something he already saw coming more clearly than I could, but he communicated it in the triple flame of the heart. A well-known monk wrote to me at the time of his death (30 December 1982): 'So Fr John has leapt into the light. I envy him. I pity you.' Over time, contradictions become paradoxes.

27 December

EACH MEMBER OF a community, or family, lives and travels together although each is at a different stage of their human journey. They connect, heal and love each other through these differences as well as their commonalities, and through their weaknesses as well as their strengths. The desire for change – and the fear it triggers – can help to bring us together. Inter-generational enrichment and sharing of wisdom cannot be part of the journey in a culture of narcissism. It requires a culture of service and generosity. Benedict calls the monastery essentially a 'school of the Lord's service' where the young respect their elders and the elders love the younger. If this is true, the goal is to make the world a monastery secured in the spirit of service.

28 December

LIKE A MULTI-FACETED diamond, the Beatitudes express all perspectives of wisdom, an integral seeing. When we struggle with a personal problem, we seek a wise person for advice. What we hope to find is not just a solution but a different way of seeing it and what its meaning is in the big picture of our life. The wise person helps us see it whole in the great perspective. When perplexed or in doubt I read the Beatitudes. They always throw an unexpected insight into the deep structures of life.

29 December

SPIRITUAL FRIENDSHIP IS a crucial element of the spiritual journey. So, if you have some understanding of the inner journey you are making, and if you have some external support, you will find what you need when you need it. You may stop the daily practice for a few weeks, months or years. I know someone who goes through a cataclysmic change every few years and throws everything out, including meditation. Then in time they remember that old hunger for something simpler and deeper, for a closer intimacy with God. They start to rummage in the pile of what they threw out and rescue the important things. We all begin. We stop. We begin again.

30 December

IN EVERY DIRECTION, meditation throws wide open the pathway to love. The first taste is a new kind of love of self which helps us live with less constantly anxious effort. Fed by love from all directions, life feels less like a struggle to survive, less of a competition. It reveals what we may have glimpsed in brief moments before, that our essential nature is joyful. Deep down, we are blissful beings. If we learn how to savour the gift of life, all the goodness and beauty it brings, we can better accept its tribulations and suffering. *Those who sow in tears will sing when they reap.* This is what we learn gently, always surprisingly but with deep gratitude, as we meditate day by day.

31 December

ENLIGHTENMENT DAWNS AS the ego sets. Fear and desire yield to the freedom to love those who challenge us with their differences and even those who cause us suffering. The miracle of non-violence replaces the sword of vengeance. Our whole person undergoes transformation from within. We taste the universal in ourselves and yielding to God as the ground of everything seems like love-play. The conflict of opposites resolves in transcendence, which is a new way and vision of life. We can serve this vision before it is fully realised in ourselves because we are more than individuals. Our great traditions teach us that there are communions of saints and that we are welcome among them. Our greatest resources are not techno-scientific but spiritual. The great teachers and lovers of humanity have not abandoned us and are not far from our wounds of inhumanity and division that they help us to heal.

References and Further Reading

My preferred biblical translation is the New English Bible (1970), although some of the quotations included here are my own version influenced by other translations.

Daily reflections are from the following by Laurence Freeman.

Books

Laurence Freeman, *Common Ground: Letters to a World Community of Meditators*, London: Continuum, 1999.
———, *Jesus, The Teacher Within*, Norwich: Canterbury Press, 2013.
———, *On Friendship*, forthcoming.

Talks

Laurence Freeman, 'Meditation Breaking the Cycle of Violence', WCCM, November 2014, https://soundcloud.com/wccm/laurence-freeman-meditation-breaking-the-cycle-of-violence.

Meditatio Talks Series (The World Community for Christian Meditation)

2005A, 'Excerpts from talks given in Singapore, Canada and USA'.
2005B, 'Excerpts from *Jesus, the Teacher Within*'.
2005C, 'UK Annual Conference, Oakham School, 1–3 April 2005'.
2005D, 'Why are we here?', https://meditatiotalks.wccm.org/cd/owY Jh3rB4eFjwFO4vKZx.
2008A, 'The Ego on our Spiritual Journey I'.
2008B, 'The Ego on our Spiritual Journey II'.
2009B, 'Spirituality in a Secular Age'.
2010B, 'The Tradition of Meditation', https://meditatiotalks.wccm. org/cd/AY20TmSk89bm4LUR04Xk.
2011C, 'Map of the Journey'.

2013A, 'Jesus and Buddha'.

2013C, 'Meditating as a Christian'.

2013D, 'Aspects of Love 1', https://meditatiotalks.wccm.org/cd/pOM dGtJWrYb8aiXY1CB6.

2014A, 'Aspects of Love 2', https://meditatiotalks.wccm.org/cd/11hd MJ5kCLeVCmpspAHv.

2014B, 'Aspects of Love 3', https://meditatiotalks.wccm.org/cd/Qn3 SG8B24bNk4jgkjEV8.

2015A, 'Health and Wholeness'.

2015C, 'Relationship with Jesus', https://meditatiotalks.wccm.org/cd/ gdpC88fo6WGR1kOv7nP3.

2017C, 'Finding Oneself 1'.

2017D, 'Finding Oneself 2', https://meditatiotalks.wccm.org/cd/84joE KuLQ5u1BznXy6dA.

2018C, 'The Experience of Being', https://meditatiotalks.wccm.org/cd/ OuXJYVwg1WeIoDCQfiUB.

2019A, 'Christian Life in the Light of Christian Meditation 1: Discipleship', https://meditatiotalks.wccm.org/cd/UgHOP8kjOsoW 9btfDhZT.

2019B, 'Christian Life in the Light of Christian Meditation 2: Holiness', https://meditatiotalks.wccm.org/cd/QBmVrdhxItHUokgBS1tQ.

2019C, 'Christian Life in the Light of Christian Meditation 3: Evangelisation', https://meditatiotalks.wccm.org/cd/aYGadOiFn68 bU496pXLl.

2019D, 'Grace at Work: The Healing Power of Meditation', https:// meditatiotalks.wccm.org/cd/P6axjep8pqrDWCjsIp2G.

2020A, 'The Work of Selfless Attention', https://meditatiotalks.wccm. org/cd/wktomfF7QFSzf5ZckG7k.

2020B, 'Contemplative Reflections on Scripture', https://meditatio-talks.wccm.org/cd/QPFR1uWtD7mtgOMo6M5s.

2021A, 'Sources of Wisdom', https://meditatiotalks.wccm.org/cd/ Viy146sRAjRzIAE86DYG.

2021B, 'Attention and Love 1', https://meditatiotalks.wccm.org/cd/ cwkSXCfLd4mxpGb6pFGc.

2021C, 'Attention and Love 2', https://meditatiotalks.wccm.org/cd/4b NGEuUCbkoQCTqGYYB2.

2021D, 'The Unconscious and Grace', https://meditatiotalks.wccm. org/cd/EQHbejZa6mkinwgNi1nH.

2022A, 'The Brick Wall of the Ego 1', https://meditatiotalks.wccm.org/ cd/aYbE1P6MprIqhknpKN5W.

2022B, 'The Brick Wall of the Ego 2', https://meditatiotalks.wccm.org/ cd/y3niOSmzZn9xooeqyWol.

2022C, 'Breakthrough', https://meditatiotalks.wccm.org/cd/TJQjSovY wKGR6hQDd598.

2022D, 'The Art of Waiting', https://meditatiotalks.wccm.org/cd/jF
DG9PMZNHmbmHOyja73.

Newsletters

Meditatio

Vol. 36, no. 3, October 2012
Vol. 37, no. 1, March 2013
Vol. 38, no. 2, July 2013
Vol. 38, no. 3, September 2014
Vol. 38, no. 2, June 2014
Vol. 38, no. 2, July 2013
Vol. 38, no. 4, December 2014
Vol. 39, no. 3, October 2015
Vol. 40, no. 1, April 2016
Vol. 40, no. 4, December 2016
Vol. 41, no. 3, October 2017
Vol. 42, no. 4, January 2019

Newsletter for the World Community for Christian Meditation

Vol. 33, no. 1, April 2009
Vol. 34, no. 3, October 2010
Vol. 45, no. 3, January 2022
Vol. 46, no. 2, February 2023

Articles

Laurence Freeman, 'Meaning', *The Tablet* (May 2015), https://us4.
campaign-archive.com/?u=c3f683a744ee71a2a6032f4bc&id
=a758cb7f05.

Also by Laurence Freeman

Beauty's Field: Seeing the world, Canterbury Press, 2014.
Christian Meditation: Your Daily Practice, Meditatio, 2014.
Contemplative Leaders: Personal Reflections by Members of the Bonnevaux Business Meditation Group, Meditatio, 2021.
The Ego on Our Spiritual Journey, Meditatio, 2008.
First Sight: The experience of faith, Bloomsbury, 2011.
John Main: The Expanding Vision, Canterbury Press, 2012.
Light Within: Meditation as Pure Prayer, Canterbury Press, 2012.

Good Work: Meditation for Personal & Organisational Transformation, Meditatio, 2019.

Inner Ecology Outer Ecology: Reflections from COP26, Meditatio, 2022.

The Inner Pilgrimage: The journey of meditation, Meditatio, 2014.

A Pearl of Great Price: Sharing the gift of meditation by starting a group, Meditatio, 2014.

The Selfless Self: Meditation and the opening of the heart, Canterbury Press, 2009.

Sensing God: Learning to Meditate through Lent, SPCK, 2015.

A Short Span of Days: Meditation and Care for the Dying, Meditatio, 2014.

A Simple Way: The Path of Christian Meditation, Medio Media, 2004.

How to Meditate

Sit down. Relax physically, releasing tension in your face muscles, forehead or shoulders. Breathe peacefully. Be aware of your incoming and outgoing breath a few times. Close your eyes lightly.

Begin to say your mantra. An ideal word is *maranatha*. It is one of the oldest Christian prayer-words, in Aramaic, the mother-tongue of Jesus. It was used perhaps as a greeting, a kind of password among early Christians. It means both 'Come Lord' and 'The Lord has come', which is a fruitful paradox. But don't think about the meaning of the word as you say it, interiorly and calmly. Listen to it as a sound, four equal syllables (ma-ra-na-tha). Don't visualise it. Sound it. Articulate the word clearly but gently and listen to the word as you say it.

Don't be discouraged by distractions. Just drop the thought or fantasy and return to the word. Learning the art of meditation is not getting rid of distractions but returning faithfully to the word.

Meditate for between 20 and 30 minutes each morning and evening. Give yourself as long as you need to build this into your daily rhythm of life.

Meditate with others often as this is very supportive to your own practice too.

If the mantra slips and you fall into distraction, return to it. If you stop meditating, start again. There is no success or failure, only being simply faithful.

'Experience is the teacher' but trust the tradition of wisdom behind what you are doing.

The mantra and the breath

It is natural to say the mantra with the breath. For example, you can say the four syllables on the in-breath and breathe out in silence. Or, many find it easier to say the first two syllables (ma-ra) breathing in and the next two (na-tha) on the out-breath. The breath is like a wheel, so you can rest the mantra lightly on it. But give your whole attention to the mantra, listening to it as you say it. As the breath slows down naturally, let the mantra be released and find its own rhythm.

Choosing the mantra and how to say it

The word I would recommend here – *maranatha* – is an ideal word because, not being in our language, it is less likely to stimulate thought or imagination. Meditation is not what you think, so don't think of its meaning but say it simply and listen to it and the silence it leads us into. It also contains primal seed-sounds associated with mantras in many traditions. If you choose another word or would like to say one in your own faith tradition, you can seek guidance from a teacher.

Above all, though, say the word faithfully, from beginning to end of the meditation session. Start saying the word again as soon as you become distracted. Say the word *until you can no longer say it* because then it has led you into a silence deeper than thought or self-consciousness. This takes time: how long depends on your practice and grace itself. We don't choose when to stop saying it but over time we say it ever more gently and subtly.

Bonnevaux Centre for Peace

Bonnevaux is the international centre of The World Community for Christian Meditation, located near Poitiers, France. It welcomes people from all backgrounds who wish to learn about meditation, to deepen their practice, to share in the life and daily work of the resident community, to engage in dialogue and immerse themselves in the silence and peace of a place where contemplation has been practised since the fifth century. There is also a programme of retreats through the year. Each day follows a rhythm of meditation, prayer, work, study, solitude and communal experience, guided by the spirit of the Rule of St Benedict.

For information on visiting and sharing in the Bonnevaux experience: bonnevauxwccm.org

Bonnevaux Centre for Peace

The World Community for Christian Meditation

The WCCM is a global contemplative family practising meditation in the Christian tradition 'in the spirit of serving the unity of all'. It is also an inclusive, multicultural network of meditation groups and teaching events, in person and online. It runs an extensive programme of online series, dialogues and special events in the annual liturgical cycle. It offers a path of accompaniment on the way of meditation from first steps to the point of sharing the gift of meditation with others. Through its inreach into the Christian world it works to restore the contemplative dimension to all kinds of Christianity. Through its outreach it works to bridge the gap between the secular and sacred and to release the wisdom of contemplative consciousness into helping us through the crisis of our time.

www.wccm.org